Speaking Aloud at Grace Church:
Homilies from the World of Willa Cather

Charles A. Peek

Speaking Aloud at Grace Church: Homilies from the World of Willa Cather
ISBN: Softcover 978- 0692628607
Copyright © 2025 by Charles A. Peek

All rights reserved. No part of this book may be reproduced or transmitted in any form or by any means, electronic or mechanical, including photocopying, recording, or by any information storage and retrieval system, without permission in writing from the publisher.

Parson's Porch Books is an imprint of Parson's Porch & Company (PP&C) in Cleveland, Tennessee. PP&C is a self-funded charity which earns money by publishing books of noted authors, representing all genres. Its face and voice is David Russell Tullock (dtullock@parsonsporch.com).

Parson's Porch & Company *turns books into bread & milk* by sharing its profits with the poor.

www.parsonsporch.com

Speaking Aloud at Grace Church:
Homilies from the World of Willa Cather

"Somehow it makes it all greater to have it all true."

> July 16, 1902 letter to Dorothy Canfield
> The Selected Letters of Willa Cather p. 63

"There is no God but one God and Art is his revealer."

> August 4, 1896 letter to Mariel Gere
> The Selected Letters of Willa Cather p. 39

"When I get through going to church and telling Indian stories I will have no more sense of truth left than [university classmate] Carlyle Tucker."

> July 27, 1896 letter to Ellen ("little Neddins") Gere
> The Selected Letters of Willa Cather p.37

Dedication

~The Three Graces~

Beverly Cooper
Barbara Sprague
Helen Stauffer

Table of Contents

Dedication 7
Acknowledgements 13
Preface 15
Foreword 17
Introduction 19

> *Photographic Plate: The Rev. Dr. L. Brent Bohlke (courtesy of Fr. Jerry Thompson, St. Marks on the Campus, Lincoln)*

Prologue 25

> Address Delivered in Grace Episcopal Church, Red Cloud, Nebraska, at a Memorial Service in Honor of the Late Willa Cather on Sunday Afternoon, November 2, 1947, by Bishop George A. Beecher, Retired Bishop of Western Nebraska. (Typescript, with changes in Bishop Beecher's own hand, from the papers of the Very Rev. George H. Peek, Dean Emeritus, St. Mark's Pro-Cathedral)

> *Photographic Plate: The Rt. Rev. George Allen Beecher (courtesy of the Archives of the Diocese of Nebraska and of Church of Our Savior, North Platte)*

The Homilies

I. "Guilty of Speaking Aloud on Christ Church Street" 32
   Cather Birthday December 7, 1999

> *Photographic Plate: Grace Church, Spring Conference 2015, with Bishop J. Scott Barker, Dr. Daryl Palmer, Dr. Steve Shively (courtesy of the Cather Collection, Willa Cather Foundation, Red Cloud)*

II. "Speaking the Truth in Love"   36
       December 27, 1992 Christmastide

III. "To Speak Well of the World"   40
       May 1, 1993 Spring Conference

IV. "Pure of Heart, Free of Judgment"   44
       April 26, 1997 Spring Conference

Photographic Plate: Church at Ácoma (personal photo)

V. "The Upward "Call"   49
       May 1, 1999 Spring Conference

VI. "Something Complete and Great"   53
       May 6, 2000 Spring Conference

VII. "Into a Complete Picture"   57
       December 7, 2000 Celebration of Cather's Birth

VIII. "Keep My Word"   60
       May 18, 2001 Spring Conference

IX. "Lowly Mangers"   65
       December 7, 2001 Celebration of Cather's Birth

X. "Coats of Many Colors"   69
       2002 Spring Conference

XI. "The Land of Enchantment"   73
       December 6, 2002 Celebration of Cather's Birth

Photographic Plate: Picasso's Guernica (personal photo)

XII. "Glimpses of Grace and Beauty"   77
       December 7, 2003 Celebration of Cather's 130th Birthday

XIII. "The Risk of Living"   83
       May 1, 2004 Spring Conference

XIV. "Dreams in the Wilderness" June 3, 2006 Spring Conference	87
XV. "Where the Sacred Is Made Known" 2007 Spring Conference	92
XVI. "Feeding the Hungry" June 2010 Spring Conference	96
XVII. "Figuratively Speaking" 2012 Spring Conference	99
XVIII. "Leave, the Lord Said" 2013 Spring Conference	105
XIX. "Providence and Plentitude" 2014 Spring Conference"	112

Photographic Plate: Grace Church, John Mallory Bates memorial window (personal photo)

XX. "Something Longer Lasting" 2015 Spring Conference	118
XXI. "Paradise Revisited" June 6, 2020 Spring Conference	125
XXII. "Lost and Found" June 3, 2023 Spring Conference	131
XXIII. "A Dwelling in which God Lives" June 7, 2025 Spring Conference	137
Epilogue "Generations" August 14, 2004 Memorial Service for Helen Cather Southwick	143

Photographic Plate: The Rev. Dr. Charles A. Peek with Dr. Steve Shively at Washington National Cathedral (personal photo)

Appendix A: "Preservation"   146
            June 2, 2006
         Celebration of the Willa Cather Prairie

     Remarks on the occasion of The Cather Foundation receiving the Cather Prairie from The Nature Conservancy

     Photographic Plate: Cather Prairie (courtesy of the Cather Collection, Willa Cather Foundation, Red Cloud)

Appendix B: brief sketch of the history of Grace Church   151
    Index (scripture, names, etc)

     Photographic Plate: Willa Cather (courtesy of the Cather Collection, Willa Cather Foundation, Red Cloud)

Acknowledgements

I am indebted to the following for invaluable help in completing these homilies for publication:

The Cather Foundation, and especially Tracy Tucker, Education Director;

The Diocese of Nebraska, and especially Jo Behrens, Archivist, as well as the Revs. Veneda Kelly, Catherine Scott, and Jerry Thompson;

The Nebraska Episcopalian, and especially Keith Winton, Editor;

And, for both encouragement and assistance, my wife, Nancy.

Preface

This book is devoted to homilies that the Rev. Dr. Charles A. Peek gave at Grace Church, Red Cloud, over the two decades spanning the turn of the 20th to the 21st Century. Dr. George Day first suggested the homilies be collected, and Fr. Peek assembled the collection with gratitude for having been asked so often to preach at Grace Church and with warm memories of the many who responded so positively over those years. Where the homilies occurred at a Spring Conference, they often emphasized particular Cather works being emphasized in the conference program. The scripture was usually drawn from the lessons assigned to a Sunday or Feast day near the time of the conference; where the scripture reference is not clear in the text, the scriptures used are listed in a footnote.

Foreword

Flannery O'Connor describes the task of a serious writer as one of noticing "lines of spiritual motion as they can be perceived on the surface of life and followed deeper into some point where revelation takes place." She continues, "This is simply an attempt to track down the Holy Ghost through a tangle of human suffering and aspiration and idiocy. It is an attempt which should be pursued with gusto."

Willa Cather certainly fulfilled O'Connor's description of a serious writer. She too sought to "track down the Holy Ghost through a tangle of human suffering and aspiration and idiocy." She did so by reading the book of experience and the embodied scripture of the lives of those who populated her world. For both O'Conner, a Roman Catholic and Cather, a Baptist who became an Episcopalian and was confirmed as such in Grace Church, Red Cloud in 1922, the world was sacramental: that is the outward and visible possesses an inner and spiritual reality, a depth that engaged them in a lifetime of searching and reporting on what they found.

Charles Peek, an Episcopal priest and a scholar with an intimate knowledge of Cather's life and work explores this "sacramental dimension" in his homilies given over the years in Grace Church. With great skill and insight, he brings in to sharp relief aspects of Cather's personal history and writing which can only deepen and expand our appreciation of what makes her novels and stories timeless in their capacity to reveal truth and the inner working of the human spirit in both its frailty and strength.

-Most Rev. Frank Griswold,
former Presiding Bishop of the Episcopal Church

Introduction

It is hard to say just how I got interested in Willa Cather. Unfortunately, it was not at the University of Nebraska, despite dancing polkas while a graduate student there with Dr. Slote. Fr. Bohlke and I frequented the same "happy hour" at the old Tony and Luigi's in Lincoln, but Cather never came up in conversation. Mine was just one of the many ways a youth can be wasted!

Dr. Helen Stauffer first invited us to Red Cloud for a Spring Conference, where we visited the Pavelka fruit cellar with no less than E. G. Marshall. Miss Bev Cooper's photographs and columns took us into Catherland, the world Mildred Bennett and her first board created to commemorate and perpetuate the life and works of Willa Cather. Barbara Sprague accompanied nearly every service I can recall and asked for a copy of every homily I gave. That is why I chose Helen, Barb, and Bev as the three "Graces"—they were my muses who introduced me to Cather and Catherland, and my love for it and them has never diminished.

I was encouraged in my involvement with Cather studies by my then Dean, Betty Becker-Theye. Betty and her husband Larry both taught at the University of Nebraska at Kearney (then Kearney State College), where Betty was Dean of Fine Arts and Humanities. When we became part of the University of Nebraska system, she was the highest ranking woman in the university system.

Later, whenever I was in Red Cloud, I'd chat with Harry Obitz, Gary Meyer, or others of the "cabinet"; Executive Directors Pat Phillips, Steve Ryan, Betty Kort, and Leslie Levy continued to invite my presence at conferences and birthday celebrations. Later, after she became the Executive Director, I was able to facilitate Betty's fine collection of Catherland photography.

My first real 'service rendered' was crouching down beside the lectern at St. Juliana, holding the votive candle from sliding off the sloping top while Steve Ryan depended on its light to speak at a candlelight service. Still later, at our first Cather Seminar at Breadloaf, Lucia Wood's photographs intrigued us with her fascinating shots of people and places. Bob Thacker's generous hospitality at the guest house there introduced us to many in the Cather community.

I became part of the Board under the Presidency of John Swift. As for scuttlebutt about the Board, I had (confession) smoke breaks with Don Conors who had been around from early on, one of the original apostles, there close to the time of "the creation." Sometimes we would meet at the headquarters of Nebraska Public Television, arranged by another benefactor of Nebraska writing and culture, Ron Hull. For security reasons, the outside door would lock behind you as you made an exit. Don and I would often have to bang on a door to get back in…a high price for sin!

If not a resident, I became at least a frequent flier to Catherland, I learned so much from the best guides a person could ever have, especially Steve Shively who also assisted with most every service I conducted at Grace Church. But, oh what a debt I owe as well to the late Merrill Skaggs and Sue Rosowski, the inimitable conference planners Bob Thacker and John Murphy, the insightful heirs to Virginia Faulkner and Berenice Slote, Janis Stout, Ann Mosely, and Ann Romines (often later accompanied by her sister Marilyn) prominent among them, and so many others who pioneered Cather studies early (Bruce Baker, Virgil Albertini, Paul Olson, and George Day) and more recent (Guy Reynolds, Mark Madigan, Richard Milligan, Evelyn Haller, Richard Harris, Evelyn Funda, Andrew Jewell, Steve Trout, and Joe Urgo). I was happy to be a "third" Charles, along with the late Charles Mignon of UNL and Chuck Johanningsmeier of UNO. Somewhere, there is a picture of us on the bridge at Avignon.

And how we have enjoyed the friendship of some of the locals, most especially the Yost family. Jay Yost served ably as both President of the Board of Governors and Executive Director, and he and his partner Wade Leak have often hosted us there, as have Dennis and Cheryl Wilson. It was through the Yosts that we first met, then came to know Tom Gallagher who more recently has led our board.

It has been especially gratifying to see the work of old-timers (think Darrel Lloyd or Robert Knoll), of the founders, and of other leaders such as Pat Phillips and Betty Kort come to fruition not long ago in the Opera House and, now, in the National Willa Cather Center, thanks in great part to a wonderful staff headed by Ashley Olson, with Tracy Tucker as our Educational Director. I can't think of a single service at Grace Church that hasn't had the assistance of someone in the office.

Grace Church has been blessed by the presence and involvement of the Episcopal Diocese of Nebraska. Former Presiding Bishop Frank Griswold gave one of the finer keynote addresses, Nebraska Bishop Joe Burnett celebrated, preached, and dedicated the Sower Award funds to improvement in the church; and the Bruce Lauritzen family (heirs to Bishop Clarkson who died returning to Omaha from Red Cloud where he celebrated his last service) continue to support the Foundation.

Bishop Clarkson

For years, services were offered at Grace by the Deans of St. Mark's Pro-Cathedral Hastings, among them my father who conducted the funeral of Carrie Miner Sherwood. Dr. L. Brent Bohlke, originally from Hastings, often conducted services and preached in Red Cloud, while variously serving congregations in York and Seward and serving as Chaplain at St. Mark's on the Campus, Lincoln. Archives of records of services are found both at the Pro-Cathedral and Diocesan Offices. Various clergy of the Diocese have joined most of our Diocesan Bishops in celebrating and preaching at Grace Church, including Ruth Jaynes and the late Jane Heenan and the late Larry Jaynes. Charles Kelliher, native to Red Cloud, joined us in a concelebration on the occasion of his 50th anniversary of his first mass, celebrated in Red Cloud. John Murphy led a Taize service here one Spring Conference. (Some of these services took place while Grace Church was still owned by the Diocese of Nebraska and housed a local congregation; others have taken place since the acquisition of the building by the State Historical Society, which subcontracts its maintenance to The Cather Foundation.)

Fr. L. Brent Bohlke

In any event, preaching to me is a communal affair, depending as much on the congregation as the preacher, on the preacher's companions and colleagues as much as the individual who speaks the words. Of these, the most constant over the years were John English and the St. Juliana singers who often sang before and during the services, and Barbara Sprague who pumped away at the old organ to accompany our song right up until her recent passing. I can still see Frank and Charlotte White singing along, having arrived with Miss Beverly Cooper!

Of course, ultimately, preaching depends on Grace, the Grace that encourages you to speak the truth in love, which is the sum of the duty of any person of any faith. Not the least of the many who conveyed God's grace to me, both in life and in preaching, is Willa Cather herself, one of the looming figures in the art of the world. What an indomitable spirit, what a sense for beauty, what a feel for good stories she adds to the cloud of witnesses!

Glimpses of God appear in the unflinching gaze of Cather's writing, and I pray the glory of both creators might occasionally shine in these homilies.

Kearney, Nebraska
Fall 2015

(1)

ADDRESS DELIVERED IN GRACE EPISCOPAL CHURCH, RED CLOUD,
NEBRASKA AT A MEMORIAL SERVICE IN HONOR OF THE LATE
WILLA CATHER ON SUNDAY AFTERNOON, NOVEMBER 2, 1947.

BY

BISHOP GEORGE A. BEECHER
RETIRED: BISHOP OF WESTERN NEBRASKA

Note: This address was delivered by Mr. O'Fallon and without the manuscript.

DEAR FRIENDS AND NEIGHBORS.

I SINCERELY HOPE THAT THIS QUIET AND PEACEFUL SERVICE IN THE
SANCTUARY OF DIVINE WORSHIP (WHERE OUR BELOVED WILLA CATHER AND
THE MEMBERS OF HER FAMILY WERE ACCUSTOMED TO WORSHIP GOD FOR MANY
YEARS;-AND WHERE, ON DECEMBER 27, 1922, I CONFIRMED WILLA CATHER AND
HER FATHER AND MOTHER) [illegible strikethrough], MAY BE
TO ALL OF US AN EXPERIENCE LONG TO BE REMEMBERED.

WE ARE IN THE OCTAVE OF ALL SAINTS' DAY AND DEAN POST, OUR
CELEBRANT OF THE HOLY COMMUNION, HAS READ THE GOSPEL STORY OF THE
BEATITUDES FROM THE FIFTH CHAPTER OF ST. MATTHEW, WHICH IS PART
OF OUR LORD'S SERMON ON THE MOUNT.

I HAVE CHOSEN THE EIGHTH VERSE OF THIS CHAPTER FOR MY TEXT:
"BLESSED ARE THE PURE IN HEART: FOR THEY SHALL SEE GOD."

WHAT THOUGHT COULD MORE VIVIDLY EXPRESS THE LIFE AND
CHARACTER OF WILLA CATHER, AS MOST OF US KNEW HER AS FRIEND-
NEIGHBOR- SCHOOL GIRL- PLAYMATE AND COMPANION.

"BLESSED ARE THE PURE IN HEART: FOR THEY SHALL SEE GOD."

FROM THE SCENES OF HER EARLIEST CHILDHOOD, SCHOOL AND
UNIVERSITY DAYS, TO THE FARTHEST REACHES OF OUR MODERN WORLD;
NO NAME IS MORE ANCHORED AMONG THE LOVERS OF CLASSIC AUTHORS THAN
THAT OF WILLA CATHER;-AND THE SOURCE OF THIS INFLUENCE LIES, NOT
ONLY IN THE FASCINATION OF HER LITERARY PRODUCTIONS,

(2)

BUT IN THE SIMPLICITY AND PRICELESS BEAUTY OF HER PERSONALITY AND CHRISTIAN CHARACTER!

BORN AND REARED IN THE ENVIRONMENT AND CULTURE OF A CHRISTIAN HOME WHERE RELIGION WAS RECOGNIZED AS THE BASIS OF THE MARRIAGE VOWS, AND WAS PRESERVED AS THE DAILY habits of that home, SHE ABSORBED THOSE ATTAINMENTS OF PURITY AND POISE WHICH, THROUGH THE YEARS BECAME THE INSPIRATION OF HER HAPPY AND USEFUL LIFE:-

LIKE NOBLE MUSIC UNTO NOBLE WORDS.

",BLESSED ARE THE PURE IN HEART: FOR THEY SHALL SEE GOD."

(1) WHEN WE WERE BAPTIZED INTO THE CONGREGATION OF CHRIST'S FLOCK, WE MADE CERTAIN DEFINITE PROMISES - EITHER OURSELVES IN OUR OWN NAME (IF WE WERE ADULTS) OR IN THE NAME OF THE CHILD BAPTIZED THROUGH THE PROMISES OF THEIR GODPARENTS. THESE PROMISES WERE FIRST "I RENOUNCE THE DEVIL AND ALL HIS WORKS, THE VAIN POMP AND GLORY OF THE WORLD, WITH ALL COVETOUS DESIRES OF THE SAME, AND THE SINFUL DESIRES OF THE FLESH, SO THAT (I) WILL NOT FOLLOW NOR BE LED BY THEM.

(2) WE PROMISED THAT WE WOULD BELIEVE ALL THE ARTICLES OF THE CHRISTIAN FAITH, AS CONTAINED IN THE EPOSTLES' CREED.

(3) WE EXPRESSED THE DESIRE TO BE BAPTIZED IN THIS FAITH.

(4) "I WILL OBEDIENTLY KEEP GOD'S WILL AND COMMANDMENTS AND WALK IN THE SAME ALL THE DAYS OF MY LIFE."

(5) WE PROMISED, EITHER OURSELVES OR THROUGH OUR GODPARENTS, "THAT WE WOULD LEARN THE CREED, THE LORD'S PRAYER, AND THE TEN COMMANDMENTS AND ALL OTHER THINGS WHICH A CHRISTIAN OUGHT TO KNOW AND BELIEVE TO HIS SOUL'S HEALTH".

(6) AMD FINALLY WE PROMISED, AS ABOVE, AS SOON AS SUFFICIENTLY INSTRUCTED, WE WOULD BE CONFIRMED BY THE BISHOP.

(3)

AS WE THINK OF WILLA CATHER, I BELIEVE THAT EVERYONE PRESENT WHO KNEW HER WILL AGREE WITH ME THAT SHE LIVED UP TO HER BAPTISMAL VOWS AS "A MEMBER OF CHRIST, THE CHILD OF GOD, AND AN INHERITOR OF THE KINGDOM OF HEAVEN".

IN MY OPINION, ONE OF HER CHIEF CHARACTERISTICS WAS HER DIS- CERNMENT OF HUMAN CHARACTER. I ONCE ASKED HER HOW SHE FELT AFTER SHE HAD FINISHED A STORY AND SUBMITTED IT FOR PUBLICATION. HER REPLY WAS, AS I REMEMBER IT, "WELL, I FEEL AS THOUGH I HAD LAUNCH- ED A PART OF MYSELF IN A BOAT AND STOOD UPON THE SHORE LONG ENOUGH TO WATCH IT DISAPPEAR INTO THE OPEN SEA."

WILLA CATHER STUDIED PEOPLE AND THEIR HIDDEN RESERVES OF POWER. SHE MAKES EVERY CHARACTER IN HER NOVELS SO REAL AND VITALLY IMPRESSIVE THAT THE READER CAN SEE AND FEEL THEIR INDIV- IDUAL CHARACTERISTICS AND PERSONALITIES TO THE MINUTEST DETAIL;- IN FACT, SHE MAKES THEM TALK -WALK -SING -DANCE AND CARRY ON THEIR CONVERSATIONS AND GAMES SO YOU CAN SEE THEIR FACES AND HEAR THEIR VOICES; ALL OF WHICH SHE TRANSLATED IN-TO STORY AND VERSE. SHE PAINTED HER PORTRAITS WITH WORDS AND SHE CERTAINLY KNEW HOW, BECAUSE THEY HAD BECOME A PART OF HERSELF. IF YOU REMEMBER THE STORY OF "MY ANTONIA" WHICH WAS AMONG HER FIRST PUBLICATIONS, SHE DESCRIBED THE NATURE OF A RATTLESNAKE IN SUCH A MANNER AS TO MAKE YOU SHIVER AND ALMOST LEAP IN THE AIR BECAUSE OF YOUR FEAR OF WHERE IT MIGHT BE AT THE TIME.

I SHALL NOT ATTEMPT TO REVIEW ANY OF HER BOOKS. THEY ALL BREATHE THE SAME SPIRIT OF WAKEFULNESS, INTENSENESS AND, AT THE SAME TIME, ARE WITHIN THE BOUNDS OF A NORMAL DES- CRIPTION.

AS I SAID AT THE BEGINNING OF MY REMARKS, WE, WHO HAVE COME TO THIS SERVICE REPRESENT WHAT I WILL CALL A GROUP OF

NEIGHBORS, DESIRING TO EXPRESS IN AUDIBLE MANNER OUR APPRECIATION OF ONE WHO, AS AN EIGHT YEAR OLD GIRL, BEGAN THE UNFOLDING OF A LIFE MISSION WITH THE ENDOWMENTS OF THAT DAILY ENVIRONMENT IN WHICH SHE GREW TO WOMANHOOD AND BECAME A UNIVERSALLY LOVED ARTIST IN THE LITERARY WORLD.

SHE PASSED HER DAYS "TRAVELING BY PONY FROM NEIGHBOR TO NEIGHBOR, SOAKING IN THE PLEASANT FLAVOR OF ALIEN WAYS". USING HER OWN WORDS I QUOTE:-"I GREW FOND OF SOME OF THE IMMIGRANTS, PARTIC- ULARLY THE OLD WOMEN, WHO USED TO TELL ME OF THEIR HOME COUNTRY. I HAVE NEVER FOUND ANY INTELLECTUAL EXCITEMENT MORE INTENSE THAN I USED TO FEEL WHEN I SPENT A MORNING WITH ONE OF THESE PIONEER WOMEN AT HER BAKING OR BUTTER MAKING. I USED TO RIDE HOME IN THE MOST UNUSUAL STATE OF EXCITEMENT."

"TWO GRANDMOTHERS IN THE CATHER HOUSEHOLD SCHOOLED THE STOCKY LITTLE GIRL IN ENGLISH LITERATURE AND FOSTERED HER INTEREST IN LATIN." *a quotation which proved to be incorrect*

AFTER GRADUATING FROM THE HIGH SCHOOL HERE IN REDCLOUD (NAMED AFTER THE SIOUX INDIAN WARRIOR) WILLA CATHER ATTENDED THE UNIVERSITY OF NEBRASKA WHERE SHE SUPPORTED HERSELF IN PART BY WORKING ON, WHAT I BELIEVE WAS, THE LINCOLN JOURNAL. SHE RE- CEIVED HER BACHELOR OF ARTS' DEGREE IN 1895.

AFTER SPENDING A YEAR OR TWO IN PITTSBURGH, PENNSYLVANIA, WORKING IN A NEWSPAPER OFFICE AND TEACHING SCHOOL, SHE BEGAN IN 1901 TO WRITE POETRY AND SHORT STORIES, WHICH SOON WERE DIS- COVERED AND PUBLISHED IN McCLURE'S MAGAZINE. DURING THE FOLLOW- ING SIX YEARS, IN 1905, SHE ENGAGED IN EDITORIAL WORK ON AN INDEPENDENT BASIS.

THIS BROUGHT HER INTO CONTACT, NOT ONLY IN NEW YORK CITY AND IN LONDON, BUT ON THE CONTINENT, WITH SOME OF THE LEADING LITERARY STARS WITH WHOM SHE BECAME PERSONALLY ACQUAINTED.

AT THIS POINT IN HER PRIMARY COURSE OF INCREASING PUBLICITY, SHE HAD THE GOOD JUDGMENT AND MOST NATURAL DESIRE TO RETURN TO HER HOME TOWN HERE IN RED CLOUD, WHERE SHE RENEWED HER FRIENDSHIP WITH THE COUNTRY PEOPLE OF HER YOUTH.
SHE LOVED THE PRAIRIE BREEZES- THE DUST OF THE WINDING TRAILS- THE GOLDEN SUN-SETS- THE FADING HORIZONS WITH THE HAPPY ANTICIPATION OF THE PROMISING DAYS AHEAD.
IN OTHER WORDS, IT WAS HOME;- AND SHE LOVED IT-; AND SHE LOVED THE PEOPLE- THE SIMPLE PLAIN TILLERS OF THE SOIL, WHO WERE BEGINNING TO MAKE THE DESERT -TO"BLOSSOM AS THE ROSE", AND THEY LOVED HER. I AM CONVINCED THAT IT WAS THIS HOMESICKNESS THAT BROUGHT FORTH THE PUBLICATION OF THE BOOK ENTITLED,-"O-PIONEERS".

FROM THIS POINT ~~IN HER CONTINUED AND VERY SUCCESSFUL PUBLICATIONS~~, SHE FOUND THE INSPIRATION FOR HER STORIES IN THE MIDWEST AND SOUTHWEST, WITH THE EXCEPTION POSSIBLY, OF THE BOOK ENTITLED "SHADOWS ON THE ROCK", WHICH WAS BASED UPON THE SCENES SHE ABSORBED FROM HER STUDY OF THE CHARACTERS IN CANADA.

AS AN ESTIMATE OF THE ASCENSION OF THE SOUL OF WILLA CATHER TOWARD HER ULTIMATE AND SUDDEN PASSING TO HER REST IN PARADISE, IT IS NOT TO BE FORGOTTEN THAT THE RECOGNITION OF HER WELL-MERITED HONORS, SHOULD BE IN SOME MEASURE, RECORDED.
IN 1931 PRINCETON UNIVERSITY, FOR THE FIRST TIME IN ITS HISTORY never having conferred it upon a woman OF ONE HUNDRED EIGHTY-FOUR YEARS, BESTOWED ON Miss Cather THE HONORARY DEGREE OF DOCTOR OF LETTERS.
SHE ALSO RECEIVED THE SAME DEGREE FROM THE UNIVERSITIES OF NEBRASKA, MICHIGAN, COLUMBIA AND YALE. LATER THE UNIVERSITY OF CALIFORNIA CONFERRED ON HER THE HONORARY DEGREE OF DOCTOR OF LAWS. IN 1933 SHE WON THE PRIX FEMINA AMERICAIN, AWARDED IN FRANCE FOR "SHADOWS ON THE ROCK".
SHE WAS A MEMBER OF THE AMERICAN ACADEMY OF ARTS AND LETTERS, AND

IN 1944 THE NATIONAL INSTITUTE OF ARTS AND LETTERS GAVE HER A GOLD MEDAL, ITS HIGHEST AWARD, IN RECOGNITION NOT OF ANY SPECIAL PIECE OF WORK, BUT OF HER GREAT ACHIEVEMENT IN LETTERS.

SURVIVING ARE TWO BROTHERS, JOHN E., OF WHITTIER, CALIF., AND JAMES CATHER, OF LONG BEACH, CALIFORNIA, AND TWO SISTERS, MRS. JESSICA AULD OF PALO ALTO, CALIFORNIA AND ELSIE MARGARET CATHER OF LINCOLN, NEBRASKA, WHO IS PRESENT TODAY IN THIS CONGREGATION AND IS SHARING WITH US THIS TRIBUTE TO HER BELOVED SISTER.

"BLESSED ARE THE PURE IN HEART: FOR THEY SHALL SEE GOD."

Bishop George Beecher

I

"Guilty of Speaking Aloud on Grace Church Street"

December 7, 1999

Cather Birthday Celebration

In 1670, a bit before Cather's time I allow, another famous American, William Penn, was arrested under statutes forbidding inciting a riot and seditious assembly. The actual reason for his arrest was the unpopularity of his minority religious views, and his judges threatened his jurors to deliver a verdict of guilty on pains of being locked up "without meat, drink, fire and tobacco." "We shall have the verdict, or you shall starve."

The jurors framed their verdict carefully...they found Penn "Guilty of speaking aloud on Grace Church Street." Not amused, the judges had them locked up in Newgate Prison. Since there is no record of their being released, if they managed to live to Old Testament ages, they may be there still. But my interest today is not in the tenacity of the jurors but in Penn and the verdict rendered of him, that he was "Guilty of speaking aloud on Grace Church Street."

Often religious and other minorities and their supporters find themselves having to speak aloud unpopular messages on and about the street where they live. This is the vocation of church and art alike. I hope today I am guilty of speaking aloud on another street by another Grace Church, but I doubt I can speak quite so aloud as Cather did. And that is what struck me as so apt for today, how Willa Cather was another who was, quite literally, "Guilty of speaking aloud on Grace Church Street."

I'm not referring specifically to her depiction of her villains, although they make a good start. One can only imagine the response of those

Red Cloud citizens who served as the models for Poison Ivy of *A Lost Lady* or Wick Cutter of *My Ántonia*. But the accuracy of Cather's gaze, the truth of her depictions came to rest on other citizens besides the rogues and fools. How unflinching is her depiction of Victoria Templeton in "Old Mrs. Harris," of the two friends, J. H. Trueman and R. E. Dillon, the two friends in the story of that title, of Jim Burden in *My Ántonia* who arrives home in May and delays visiting his disgraced friend Ántonia until he's ready to return to school in the fall, of Marian Forrester whose luster becomes tarnished in Niel's eyes after he discovers her attraction to a succession of scoundrels. And since we know a good deal of Cather's writing was autobiographical, characters and events arising out of her own family experience, what must her family have thought of her veiled depictions of them?

That's the way with art: it shakes our world, our way of seeing it and ourselves, to the foundations. When we read and read truly, something very akin to Peter's description in our lesson today takes place: "the heavens disappear with a great rushing sound, the elements disintegrate, and the earth with all that is in it is laid bare" (II Peter 3, NEV).

And we, so depicted, don't generally like the way we look when we appear transformed into the characters of a novel. The citizens of Oxford, Mississippi didn't much care for Faulkner; we can imagine similar apprehensions here in Red Cloud about Cather. The novelist of the great prairie and desert West gave the prairie and desert citizens much to reflect on, much to fear, much to rue. She "spoke aloud" on her Grace Church street, in her America and its habit of not well-honoring those who speak aloud the truth about us.

Russians may have lined up by the tens of thousands for Tolstoy's funeral cortege, but in America, we like to bury our authors off somewhere safe, glad to have their books after they are no longer so directly identifiable with our place and time; the books on the shelves, and good riddance to the writers.

Red Cloud and her experience her as a young person of the new western civilization then in the making stuck with Willa all her life, and she spent that life, whether in the classroom or at *McClure's* or in the novels and stories, turning her unflinching gaze on what life had taught her to observe wherever she went, and she continued until her death "speaking aloud" or later from Grace Church street.

Guilty as charged! And because guilty, one of our great, enduring modern prophetic voices, like Penn's or like Isaiah's. And what of it? Peter directs us to the point: Since the whole universe as we thought we knew it is to break up, or in Isaiah's words, since every valley is being lifted up and every mountain and hill brought down and the rugged places made smooth ad the mountain ranges turned into plains and even the flowers fade when the spirit of God blows over them—since, in a word, we can never see ourselves or our world the same again, then, asks St. Peter, "what sort of people ought we to be"?

That's the way with those who "speak aloud on Grace Church Street": they leave it all in our lap! Whether we will be the sort of people who speak aloud in our turn, will resist the tyrannies of our own days, will give something of our lives to those who do, and are willing to risk our meat and drink and fire and tobacco for something worthwhile.

Willa Cather knew how the world as we think we know it can disintegrate, can, as she put it, break in two; knew what were the enduring truths that survived; and of it all spoke aloud on, of, from, and about Grace Church Street. Guilty as charged, thank God! Happy Birthday, Willa. And now, what sort of people ought we to be?

Bishop J. Scott Barker celebrates at the 2015 Spring Conference with Daryl Palmer and Steve Shively, assisting.

II

"Speaking the Truth in Love"

December 27, 1992

Christmastide[1]

I want to set the scene tonight by calling our attention to a sentiment expressed in one of Cather's most enduring plains novels. During the search for a suitable place to bury Mr. Shimerda in her *My Ántonia*, Jim's grandmother becomes indignant at the sectarian intolerance they encounter. "If these foreigners are so clannish," she exclaims to Mr. Bushy, "we'll have to have an American graveyard that will be more liberal-minded" (Houghton Mifflin 73).

December 27, 1992, will mark the 70th anniversary of Cather's confirmation here at Grace Church by Bishop George Allen Beecher, a bishop who, as Carrol Simcox once noted, was the only "apostolic presence" in the procession of the House of Bishops.[2]

I must confess that I can't imagine that Confirmation meant much "theological" assent on Willa's part. Her fiction seems to suggest a decided lack of interest in ecclesiastical organization or doctrinal quarrels, and this might explain why she chose to be confirmed in a

---

[1] Scripture for this homily was taken from I John 1:1+ and John 21:19 (the lessons in the 1928 *Book of Common Prayer* for the feast of St. John the Evangelist) and from Amos 7:17-17, Matthew 22:34-46

[2] Interestingly, at the time of this writing, scholars have raised the issue of Cather's Baptism, there seeming to be no place where any such baptism was registered, although it is alluded to in the typescript of Bp. Beecher's homily at Cather's memorial service.

"non-confessional" church, i.e. one whose catechism is subordinate to its common prayer.[3]

But Grandma Burden's comment may give us a focus for the spiritual connections to which Cather's Confirmation seems to have been a witness. It shows an awareness (similar to Whitman's) that a new world meant a new start, with less to divide us, more call to accept one another! (One could hardly argue against the proposition that we need a lot more of that attitude in our own day!)

An attitude similar to the one expressed by Grandma Burden seems to be illustrated in Cather's choice to attend Church of the Ascension, lower 5th Avenue, New York City. [4]

That choice might suggest Cather's love of the beautiful. She might well have been fond of its architecture, music, and art, especially the lovely John Lafarge mural of Christ's Ascension that looms over the altar there.

The choice may equally well presage Cather's love of Truth; Percy Grant was one of the clergy there and was known, as a broad churchman, to be outspoken about the Gospel message.

And, similarly, she may have been attracted there by her allegiance to The Good, in this case to the social outreach for which not only Ascension but also the neighborhood was known. For instance, the first day care center for working mothers in New York City was only one block from Cather's apartment in Greenwich Village.[5]

With her classical education, echoed in that of Jim Burden, it is a safe assumption that Cather was well aware of the Greek Trinity: The

---

[3] While the Reformation and Counter Reformation were beating out doctrinal statements, Anglicans were busily producing *The Book of Common Prayer* . . . a good thing, too, since when we aren't praying we trend toward being contentious!

[4] Bearing out Cather's lack of interest in institutional affiliation, Church of the Ascension records bear no mention of her membership there.

[5] Years later, with Jewell and Stout's publication of her letters, we find iterations of her concern for what we would call social welfare and would then have been known as the social gospel

Good, The True, and The Beautiful, but I doubt they were compartmentalized in Cather's mind. They might well have come together in a term favored by Anglican's, the term "lovingkindness."

That same set of values was often found as well in the "minority report" of the neighboring Hebrew culture, the words of the prophets. Amos, for instance, confronting both the entrenched nepotism of the "prophet class" and the larger loss of values in which new ways were nothing but old wrongs, had to both assert the value of truth over one's lineage and reassert a standard of goodness and truth "I am no prophet, nor a prophet's son, but I am a herdsman, and a dresser of sycamore trees, and the Lord took me from following the flock, and the Lord said to me, 'Go prophesy to my people." And what is his prophetic vision? "Behold I am setting a plumb line in the midst of my people."

Similarly, Jesus, confronting myriad demands and opinions of various sects of his day, could see the law intended to lead us to love was instead taking the place of love, the keeping of the law becoming pride in the imagination of our hearts. Like the poet Yeats, he could see "the ceremony of innocence drowned."

Asked the greatest commandment, Jesus replied, "Love the Lord your God with all your heart, and with all your soul, and with all your mind. This is the great and first commandment. And a second is like it . . . love your neighbor as yourself."

This insistence that we not "major in the minors," that we stick to fundamental goodness, truth, and beauty, will not sound at all strange to readers of Cather, readers familiar with how she often depicts a society where the stratification of rules, regulations, and respectability had replaced the initial equalities of the new west. The political and economic had replaced the personal and humane. Ugliness had overshadowed beauty, banality overcome quality.

Dealing with people who, in her generation, had increasingly claimed 'necessity' to excuse what was sheer 'expediency,' Cather sought to depict the past in such depth as would reveal what was truly necessity and what was merely greed and exploitation.

It was to highlight these themes that I chose the scripture for today, lessons fit for celebrating the birth of a woman who was no prophet nor any prophet's daughter but who told the truth nonetheless, who set a plumb line among us that will tell the truth about us.

George MacDonald called the day we die the first in a happier series of birthdays. Today, in honor of the birthday of one already happier, let us celebrate her truthfulness and, so, find truth in her celebration of the simple goodness and beauty of the people and place she knew so well.

III

"To Speak Well of the World"

May 1, 1993

Spring Conference

Cather continually focuses the reader of *A Lost Lady* on the lost west, the west first imperiled and then lost through the development of caste and class. Many things may have contributed to the brief life of the frontier west, not least the incursion and presence of the pioneering east and its more or less habitual divisions of caste and class, depicted in *A Lost Lady* beginning in chapter one.

Often disregarded or discounted by scholars as a major focus of Cather's writing (as well as a major concern of Cather's personally and professionally), the depiction of how artificial social divisions destroy freedom and dignity forms a major part of her work, and nowhere more than in *A Lost Lady*.

One focus of this concern is Captain Forrester, seen in the novel as the great pioneer. At one point, the narrator, watching Niel follow Daniel Forrester's slow progress on two canes, remarks, "He looked like an old tree walking" (115). This would be a strange simile if it were not a direct allusion to an equally strange parallel from the Gospel of Mark, where the context enlightens us as to Cather's use of the allusion.

They came to Bethsaida. And some people brought to him a blind man, and begged him to touch him. And he took the blind man by the hand, and led him out of the village; and when he had spit on his eyes and laid his hands upon him, he asked him, 'Do you see anything?' And he looked up and said, 'I see men; but they look like trees, walking.' Then again he lad his hands upon his eyes; and he looked intently and was restored, and saw everything clearly. And he sent him away to his home, saying, 'Do not even enter the village' (Mark 8:22-26 RSV).

(There is, incidentally, a parallel passage in Matthew's Gospel where, instead of spit, Jesus is said to use mud. The use of spit or mud becomes almost a trope, such that one often hears homilies that conflate the two stories, confusing the two.)

The allusion, of course, is to the moment between the two phases of the man's sight being restored, the moment when he sees men but they look like walking trees, but the allusion is only a means to an end, the means of drawing the full healing story to bear on *A Lost Lady*, for the outline of the biblical story is woven into Cather's account of Niel and Mrs. Forrester.

Twice, each time positioning Niel as a voyeur to a scene, thus keeping the motif of sight in front of the reader, Niel encounters Mrs. Forrester in the embrace of some man not her husband, once Frank Ellinger, then Poison Ivy. Each encounter is an "eye-opener" for Niel, who begins to marvel at how well the Captain knows his wife. Between the two eye-openers, Cather places the remark about Captain Forrester appearing like a tree walking. That is, Cather places the remark in the novel just where it is placed in the biblical story, between two phases of a process of eye opening.

After the first encounter, Niel throws the flowers he has picked into the mud, and after the second he retraces his steps by that mud where he had thrown the flowers the first time. As if the introduction of the spit/mud motif would possibly still not be enough, Cather gives us a glimpse into what Niel is thinking, "It took two doses to cure him. Well, he had had them" (170).

And there is still a bit more. In Mark the strange healing falls between two misunderstandings, two blindnesses if you will: the disciples' failure to understand the meaning of the feeding of the 5000 on the one hand and their similar failure to understand the nature or necessity of Jesus' own suffering. Similarly, in Cather's novel Niel's eye-opening encounters fall between Mrs. Forrester feeding the boys in the grove on the one hand and her own suffering on the other.

Niel misunderstands both of these scenes in some significant way. This of course makes Mrs. Forrester the "Christ figure" of the novel and Niel the "blind" disciple.

Now all literary allusions have their limits. Here, Cather inscribes the scriptural text into her own, not for many of the biblical themes but only for one...not for instance for any theme of 'holiness' or moral ideals, but only for the applicability of the themes of blindness and sightedness.

The allusion is one of the many ways we readers are alerted to how *A Lost Lady* is a novel of many blindnesses. There is Niel's blindness to seeing any individuality in the other boys, to seeing anything genuine in the townswomen's concern for Marion, to seeing Marion age; blindness to the fact of her fears or to accepting them as part of her, to seeing how the past might apply to the present, or to seeing the sexuality of Marion Forrester; blindness especially to grasping with any comprehension her "power to live" (125, 171).

But Niel's are not the only instances of blindness. There is also the blindness of the upper classes to the plight of the lower, the blindness of the lower classes to the artificiality of the barriers which exclude them (as for instance when Adolph 'wouldn't come to the funeral' (145). And what of the blindness of the other stock-holders to their duty when the financial institution fails? What of the blindness of supposed old friends to Mrs. Forrester's subsequent needs?

Indeed, *A Lost Lady* is a veritable catalog of ways to be blind, all emblemized in the little bird Ivy Peters blinds. We see the malice of the act before we understand how it provides emphasis to the portraits of the willing blindness of the human participants to the novel's action. How often, as in Niel's averted gaze, they seem to fear clear sight. Like Sgt. Schultz of the old sitcom *Hogan's Heroes*, they "see nothing." But here, the Schultzes are not very loveable and the situation is far from comic.

The novel couples blindness and fear in the tension known in small towns and small neighborhoods, the tension between knowing (even nosing around) so much, and yet fearing what we will see, who will see us, what the neighbors will think, how seeing will lead to judging.

All this blindness is played off in the novel with the comments about and instances of Captain Forrester's clear-sightedness. As the structural counterpoint shows the dangers of blindness and commends the benefits of sight, the rhetoric of the novel serves to draw the reader into scorning blindness and coming to a new appreciation of sight.

I am reminded of a wonderful Annie Dillard essay on 'sight and insight,' where she discusses the case of people who have been blind and, then, through surgery, begin to recover their sight—about how they come to see and how they value seeing. A student of mine, working recently on that essay, was struck by Dillard's description how such people at first see objects and their shadows as "color-patches" and "dark marks." He wrote in his response statement to his reading, "Those people have taught me to see the world as a dazzle . . . We need to express what we see . . . blurt out the . . . words, oh God! How beautiful! We need to speak well of the world." Surely, a very similar response follows a close reading of *A Lost Lady*.

Cather starts with what seems given, the blindness, especially that of others, as seen by Niel. But, in a formula she perfected in *My Ántonia*, we then learn something of Niel's own blindness. And that, in turn, in a kind of double effect, leads us to question his reliability, the question the credibility of his view of the blindness of others. The reader, too, receives "two doses," one healing in two phases. *A Lost Lady* and the scripture inscribed in it, the Christ of the Gospel and the Christ-figure of the novel, call us to take a second look, not to be satisfied with what things look like, to pierce through the veil to what things really are.

The novel may tell a very personal and domestic story, but that story is a call to look again at the perennial problem of caste and class, the plague that stalked at the high-noon of the frontier west, and still plagues us in the noonday of our own times.

IV

"Pure of Heart, Free of Judgment"

April 26, 1997

Spring Conference

I'd like to invite you to make with me three brief church visits.

The first will be to the ancient church in Ácoma as Cather describes it in *Death Comes for the Archbishop:*

> At the very edge of the mesa, overhanging the abyss so that its retaining wall was like a part of the cliff itself, was the old warlike church of Ácoma, with its two stone towers. Gaunt, grim, grey, its nave rising some seventy feet to a sagging, half-ruined roof, it was more like a fortress than a place of worship. (100)

Here is a photograph of the same church as I saw it in an excursion to Ácoma with participants in a Western Literature Association conference:

Having seen the church, let me now proceed to ask you to note with me another subtle quality of Cather's characterizations in *Death Comes for the Archbishop*.

Through descriptions tinged, some with ambiguity, some with irony, Cather raises a profound question for the reader. Just as she notes that no one could quite tell the origin of the church's decoration—is it of Spanish or Native origin?—so she suggests no one can be sure about the origin and spirit of the whole design of the Spanish missionary project.

By now, of course, partly due to writers and historians, Cather not least among them, we are accustomed to the tension between the two heritages, between the designs of the explorers/discoverers/conquerors (even how we label them having evolved in time) and the culture of the natives who lived in North and South America in roughly equal numbers to those living in Europe.

There is an apocryphal story of a traveler in the Southwest who suffers a blowout of a tire. Seemingly out of nowhere, a local of indeterminate race appears and aids in changing the tire so the traveler can go on his way. As he looks back in his rear view mirror, the native helper is nowhere to be seen. The driver recalls vividly their last exchange, when he asked "What do I owe you?" and the mysterious helper replied, "You don't know yet!"

Cather, as writer, as artist in words, seems always supremely aware of what we don't know yet. Here is another challenge to add to our list: it is entirely possible that Bp. Latour is not, at least not in any conventional sense, the hero of *Death Comes for the Archbishop*. We might, following her lead, ask, in what does he actually succeed? The original mission or some mission that evolves from his interaction with the local scene? The erection of the stone cathedral? Yes, but only after letting native history cast doubts on the efficacy of taking refuge on the rock!

And how much does Latour know of the people Fr. Joseph knows? And which of their funerals is a sold-out SRO affair?

I am not belittling the great Bishop by suggesting that the novel itself suggests that there are many ways death comes for us, and that sometimes this is in the death of our earliest dreams. Possibly, as in Shakespeare, we find in Jean Latour, for some time before he dies, a grave man, given to question some of the premises on which his life has been based.

And yet, there is no question that Cather treats lovingly and tolerantly the Bishop, as indeed she does most of the folk of *Death Comes for the Archbishop*, our author not rushing to judgment of the natives as did the Spanish, not rushing to judgment of the Spanish as do we.

So much for our first church visit. Our second visit is here, to this church, Grace Church, joining those who came here on All Souls Day, 1947, with those who gathered for Cather's memorial. It was in this place and on that day that another Bishop, Bishop George Beecher, also captured this quality in Cather.

His text for that day was "blessed, the pure in heart" and the good Bishop did his listeners the favor of not misconstruing that scripture to refer to something about Willa Cather's manners or morals. He was too close to Cather, and had too much feeling for her, for that. Instead, he went straight to the point, the artist's heart which, like God, held all things in love and was thus pure, pure in heart, free of judgment, willing (as Kierkegaard would have had it) one thing only...the good of her creation.

So, first the ancient church in Ácoma, then this very precious little prairie church that once served God by welcoming one of the great spirits of its times, and now a third and final visit, one perhaps you've made before, perhaps not, a visit to this or that church, any church, after it has emptied, as perhaps on the day after a great celebration such as Easter Sunday or Christmas Eve.

On this visit, you may occasionally hear the creak of a floorboard, the groaning of the shell of the edifice. Otherwise, you will be left where moments of emptiness and silence often leave us—left wondering. Sometimes, you know, we, too, feel our shell just encloses a great empty hole. Sometimes the empty building mirrors a true but unspoken feeling, one most present a moments of pain or loss, the feeling that possibly God, too, is absent, that the church surrounds nothing more than a mere myth made up to still our fears. Still, let's not cut too short this visit, this quiet, almost intrusive visit when, in our mind's eye, the roof and walls enclose only empty space and silence.

I have given members and guests many tours here at Grace Church, as I have many other churches; I don't recall any when I took the occasion to point to the most pervasive, persistent feature of almost any church: the silence, the emptiness, which form most often its atmosphere.

But picture yourself in such a church, perhaps especially in this church, alone and still in the silence and unoccupied space, and think for a moment how the silence has seen and the emptiness enclosed so many good people: people devoted to family and community, scholars searching for the truth and beauty to be found in Cather's works, the Cather Foundation's founder, Mildred Bennett, and its early preacher, Fr. Brent Bohlke; think of all the pious, devout, and spiritual people, perhaps members of Cather's day, perhaps visitors since; think of what great love, valor, and virtue those good people showed the world and found here in others.

Now, you may also have had the thought that, truth be known, that silence has seen, that emptiness has closed round so many bad people, too: some gossips and idlers, some slicksters and boosters, some who were covetous, envious, and arrogant, quite possibly if Cather's fiction is any guide, here and there a murderer, a thief, an exploiter of others for pleasure or profit. I'm sure the walls could tell their stories.

But here's the most amazing truth: the bad people the emptiness closed round, the good people the silence saw . . . were the same people. What else in the face of that amazing fact of human nature could you expect except an emptiness that bids us junk our judgments and judgmentalism and a silence that bids us be still and listen for God, the empty church bidding us as did the psalmist: "for God alone my soul in silence waits" (Psalm 62:1)!
But have we not just come upon one of Cather's great discoveries as

an artist? Did she not find that silence which is simply the refusal to judge? The great 20th Century philosopher Ludwig Wittgenstein remarked that about that which we cannot speak we must remain silent. Like us, rooves and walls shut out as much as they hold in, but the emptiness makes room for all.

Cather championed a certain art, so well exemplified in *Death Comes for the Archbishop*: an art of that which is left unsaid, an art with room for emptiness, room left by uncluttering the house of its unneeded furnishings, the same emptiness as the emptiness of the tomb on Easter morning, a silence and emptiness not so much features of a building as characteristics of a soul, such silence and emptiness as comprise the purity of heart Bishop Beecher found to praise in Willa Cather.

V

"The Upward Call"

May 1, 1999

Spring Conference

In our Gospel (John 14:8-14), Jesus gives his listeners what may at first sound like a strange alternative.

First, he says, "Believe me that I am in the father and the Father in me."

That's not so strange—that's what we've come to see Christian believing is all about, the assent to a unique relationship between God (creator, spirit, perfect love) and this man, Jesus (son of Man, son of God, Messiah, Christ). This is the confession of faith.

But then Jesus says, "or else believe me for the sake of the works themselves." We aren't prepared for this alternative at all, not even prepared for there to be an alternative!

But here it is, a pragmatic basis for an alliance of sorts. If you see work that impresses you, this is a tie to the worker; if you want to do such work—or even greater work—come on board.

But the paradoxical invitation isn't so paradoxical after all:

There are Jews and then there are Jews, just as there are Christians and then there are Christians. Among Jesus' listeners were devout and pious Jews, traditionalists, whose roots were in the Torah and its revelation of God the father who would one day send a Messiah to redeem Israel. To them Jesus bids: Believe me that I am in the Father and the Father in me."

But there were also cosmopolitan Jews, Jews with much contact with Greco-Roman thought, and even non-Jews, those whom Peter refers to elsewhere as "those in every nation who fear God and do what is right" (Acts 10:35). To them his appeal is to the works whose quality and aim they could share.

Now, I don't know—can't know—about Willa Cather and the former part of the invitation. She belonged and attended church; its symbols and practices seemed to have great value for her, not only personally but also as an author. She belonged here and adorned this church. That she was eclectic, we can imagine: raised a Baptist, becoming an Episcopalian, admiring Roman Catholicism. She seemed to grow spiritually all her life. The state of her inner belief we cannot know. But of her relationship to the latter invitation, to believe because of the works—the works he did and the works she would do—I haven't the slightest reason to doubt.[6]

Jesus was offering what some came to term "the upward call." That upward call—that was Cather. She heard it all her life and it infuses her works. You can hear it in how she constructs Jim Laird's description of Harvey Merrick in "The Sculptor's Funeral": "off there in the world, away from all this hogwallow, climbing the big, clean up-grade he'd set for himself" (*Collected Stories* 209-10). You can hear it in her essay "The Education You Have to Fight For," when she refers to teaching in the early days of prairie life as "a kind of missionary work, a solemn duty." Caught in the bleakness of prairie life in those early days, she tells us "boys and girls thought about it and dreamed about it." And she speaks of the quality education touched in them as "a kind of fire, a really burning ambition and devotion." That same calling upward from their circumstances, that same lighting of a fire of devotion in the hearts of good people, that same zeal to help people see the light—these all can be seen in every aspect of her work.

Now, Cather wasn't parochial. So far as we know, she sought no partisan following even for the religion she practiced; but she did know how truth raises us up, did know how the inspiration of

---

[6] Comments in the *Letters*, not available at the time of the preaching, would confirm Cather's respect for the moral and social results of faith.

goodness and beauty propels us higher. To these she tried to be true and these she tried to convey in her every word.

I was so impressed with her portrait of young learners and teachers out in the prairie schools and new universities. She was showing great insight when she said of those institutions, "What they are to be depends on the young men and women who study in them and who teach in them."

It's with this thought that I recall one of the most vivid experiences of my life.

Dr. Stuart Embury of Holdrege invited me to Haiti for a surgical mission. We spent over a week there in a surgery at a Wesleyan mission on the island of La Gonave, the island you see out in the jaws of Haiti when you look at a map. A high, cement-block wall surrounded the mission compound. On my first night there, I wandered out into the compound and looked down toward its end where two tall poles held aloft the only electric lights in the entire village after 10:00 p.m. And looking that direction I noticed strange little humps above the top of the wall. There was a slight mound at one point in the compound and I thought, if I could get to the top of that mound, I could see over the wall and discover what caused those humps. When I got up on the mound, I saw that the far side of the wall was crowded with youngsters, standing in the dust of the alley, their backs to the wall, each with a book. They were trying to read their lessons by the only lights available to them.[7]

Many times I have wanted to relive that experience, but, as Cather knew, most of our really vital experiences can't be relived, can't be repeated. "Omnes optima fugit" she inscribed as the epigram of *My Antonia*. But even lived only once, these are the moments that light that fire, drive that devotion, instill that zeal. And where they are limited in our living of them, we have unlimited access to them in

---

[7] As of the composition of this book of homilies, Dr. Embury is still taking teams to Haiti, adults and youth, medical professionals and others. His vast collection of Art History resides next to the Cather collection in the University of Nebraska Love Library Archives.

the stories of great authors like Cather. There we can have recourse to them again and again, refueling that fire, recharging our batteries, renewing our zeal.

Think of the power of words, of works of literature to issue and effect that upward call, that belief for the sake of the works that inspire us to our own works.

You know, for a life like Cather's, if the Roman Catholics were handling this, you can imagine someone trying to get her canonized. I know there is that technicality that there have to have been at least three bona fide miracles. But if *O Pioneers!* and *Death Comes for the Archbishop* and *The Professor's House* and "Old Mrs. Harris" and "The Sculptor's Funeral" aren't miracles, then I don't know what one is. And that's plenty more than are required and it would not be hard to add to our list.

Jesus said, "[S]he who believes in me will also do the works…and greater works than these will [s]he do…whatever you ask in my name, I will do it." Cather apparently asked, and it was done. Works and greater works poured from her pen. And here today, whether or not we believe Jesus was in the Father and the Father in Him, perhaps we, too, can believe for the sake of the works.

VI

"Something Complete and Great"

May 6, 2000

Spring Conference

I have chosen for today a gospel lesson that was read in many churches around the world this past Sunday, the Second Sunday of Easter for those who keep the calendar, Low Sunday for those who count the dwindled attendance after the second feature of the Poinsettia – Lily Fixation. And for the epistle, a scripture that same calendar assigns for tomorrow.[8]

I chose them in part for the theme announced in John's letter and in part for the encounter related by John's Gospel. John announces, "Our theme is the word of life. This life was made manifest." The followers had experienced life itself in their midst, visible, palpable. I love how John cuts through the theologies of who Christ was, ignores the various explanations of how He could have been who He was, and goes right to the simple and profound comment: somehow the very thing that makes life joyous and makes joy meaningful became visible. And his invitation to join in that life echoes in Cather's own comments on life, for instance when she has Jim Burden say "That is happiness, to be dissolved into something complete and great" (*My Ántonia*). Jim's words could be a text for this morning; in fact…they are! It is a text suggested to me by Steve Shively.

And I suspect Cather would have liked as well John's rendition of Jesus' encounter with Thomas, often dubbed the doubter: but that demeans Thomas only to those who think that doubt is the opposite of faith. Yet here, in this story, Thomas' doubt is precisely his

---

[8] The Epistle: I John 1:1-2:2; the Gospel: John 20:19-31

insistence that the figure standing before him not be some conjurer's trick. Jesus had predicted that the Son of Man must *first* suffer and *then* rise. That is all humanity's question: is suffering the whole story, or do the suffering rise? Is there any truth that the first shall be last and the last first? Thomas didn't want a Jesus who got *around* suffering; he wanted one, if one existed, who had gotten *through* it.

And that, as I read the scripture, is its great promise. The Kingdom of God is a place of transfers and reversals, a site of a radical redistribution of spiritual assets from where some people, often religious people, think they belong. The barren conceive, the old give birth, the lame walk, the blind see. In the story of Jesus' crucifixion and resurrection we see that in God's kingdom things cast down are raised up, things grown old are made new, and all things are brought to their perfection. The accounts of Jesus' passion drive this home through every little detail, each a transfer, a reversal: the garment Jesus wore is transferred to the soldiers, the cross offered his followers is placed on the back of a stranger, the treasury once in Judas' charge passes on to James, the confession once on Peter's lips is voiced by the centurion. Jesus transfers the care of Mary and John to one another, he moves from the intimate companionship of Bethany with Mary and Martha and Lazarus to the companionship of thieves, one of whom is transferred from the cross to paradise, and Jesus, the property of the poor, is transferred to the tomb of the rich. That's the scripture's story and Thomas knows it...no wonder he wants to see wounds. And because of his insistence, he recognizes them as the healed wounds of the wounded healer.

Now, this particular focus bears directly on Cather and her work. The Rev. Dr. Brent Bohlke and I used to wonder how it was that Willa Cather chose New York's Church of the Ascension for her home parish. It was, after all, as Brent reasoned it, a parish firmly planted in what was then called "the social gospel," and Brent assumed that the very private Cather wouldn't much have cared for the social gospel. So, he guessed it must have had something to do with how the LaFarge mural depicting the Ascension behind the altar at Church of the Ascension appealed to Cather, the artist. As was almost always the case with Brent, this is a reasonable view. However, in this case, the philosophy of the parish, indeed the very subject the mural depicts, were no accident and I don't think they were separated in Cather's mind.

About the time Cather wrote and published her major works, there surrounded her a veritable religious war. On one side of this war were folks then called "dispensational premillennialists," under the influence of John Nelson Darby and his disciple C. I. Scofield. Perhaps you've never heard of them, but that's all right because I doubt you've heard of Walter Rauschenbusch either and he led the other side, he and someone you may well have heard of named Henry Emerson Fosdick. And whether or not we've heard of them, Rauschenbusch was historically important for his influence on the thinking of Gandhi and Martin Luther King, Jr., and Desmond Tutu.

It's not my intention this morning to engage in their nearly century old debate, but the tenets of Rauschenbusch and Fosdick will interest you as students of Cather. Opposing too many Christians who sought to save their souls but didn't care about the condition of our world, Rauschenbusch wrote, "The better we know Jesus, the more social do his thoughts and aims become" because the Kingdom of God "is not a matter of getting individuals into heaven but of transforming . . . life on earth into the harmony of heaven." Opposing those who were more concerned with doctrinal correctness than with their neighbor, Fosdick would add, "There are many opinions in the field of modern controversy concerning which I am not sure whether they are right or wrong, but there is one thing I am sure of: courtesy and kindliness and tolerance and humility and fairness are right. Opinions may be mistaken; love never is."

Now these views of Rauschenbusch and Fosdick, were precisely those called "the social gospel," the gospel preached at Church of the Ascension. And they sound like views Cather would find congenial to her own thinking. They certainly sound like the philosophy behind her works, the philosophy we glimpse behind her poignant depiction of Erik Hermannson's soul, behind Grandmother Burden calling for a "more American" graveyard not so fussy about who is buried there, behind the raising up of the cast down Ántonia, and, again, behind the revelation expressed by Jim Burden: "That is happiness, to be dissolved into something complete and great."

Cather's affinity for these views may well explain why she seems often to have attended services at Church of the Ascension. Always a keen student, Cather would have been aware of the social gospel and its advocates from the *New York Times* which carried almost weekly articles and editorials on it. And surely with her artist's eye, it would not have escaped Cather's attention that the social gospel philosophy was captured in the depiction in the mural behind the altar. She must have seen how the two pictures of Christ being lifted up, once on the cross and once into heaven, form the meaning of the faith based on Easter, of a gospel of love with the power to transform life on earth, its promise of life to all who lose their lives, whose lives are dissolved into something complete and great.

Jesus' invitation today to touch his wounds is an invitation to see the cross as the way of life, to view it as the seal upon all that is sacrificed for what is noble and good, as the proof that God's light shines and God's love is real and God's world awaits those who believe every darkness should be lit and every loneliness loved. It is an invitation Cather seems to have accepted. And if she didn't receive and accept that invitation only or first at Church of the Ascension, she seems to have received it and accepted it there regularly, and most certainly translated its message into her stories that the world so loves.

VII

"Into a Complete Picture"

December 7, 2000

Cather Birthday Celebration

Early in my life, my mother taught me a little verse I eventually learned was from English poetry: "Oh, what a tangled web we weave, when first we practice to deceive." As I grew up, I learned that the warp and woof of human experience can get pretty tangled even without practice or deception. And so I became one of those people who is always amazed at folks who have all the truth, who trust completely in how they see things. This amazes me because all of life seems to tell us how partial is our vision, how dark the glass through or into which we look. My experience, at least, is full of reminders of how I missed the signs.

Luke captures this in our reading this morning from his gospel (Luke 3). He makes sure at the outset that we see all the things everyone would have paid attention to, the figures who, had they had evening news, would have appeared in it: the 15th year of Tiberius Caesar's reign, Pontius Pilate being governor of Judea, Herod being Tetrarch of Galilee, Annas and Caiaphas the High Priests. But then he shifts to what the evening news would have missed: Zechariah and John, over in the Jordan backwater, and the news that, not out of the corridors of power but in the voice crying in the wilderness, the valleys were about to fill up, the mountains about to be brought low, and the crooked made straight. Whoever the know-it-alls of that day were, this is what they would have missed.

In my church, the Episcopal Church, we have begun the season called Advent, and Advent begins for us with a prayer to "cast away the works of darkness and put on the armor of light." No wonder we pray so: we walk so often in darkness, a little light could surely help.

This was in my thoughts lately when I turned for my weekly reading of Miss Beverly J. Cooper's "As I Grow Older," a pleasure made possible by the gift of receiving the *Red Cloud Chief*. In one column, Beverly tells of her distant cousin, Leslie Hoff, and how, out on the town in New York just before shipping out to North Africa, his group of fellows encounters two girls emerging in the rain from the subway and strike up a conversation with them. One of them was Elsie Vagoda. Three years of only letters later, Leslie and Elsie were married upon Leslie's discharge. Beverly concludes her story with a question: "Our lives are more than coincidences, aren't they?"

Archbishop Temple was once confronted by a journalist who, knowing Temple's intellect, asked him, "Archbishop, don't you really believe that what we call answers to prayers are really only coincidences?" "Why, yes," Temple replied. "I do. And I've noticed something else," he added; "when I quit praying, the coincidences stop happening."

Monday, a group of English majors and I finished reading together Willa Cather's *Sapphira and the Slave Girl*. The very title of the novel rubs our noses in the character who dominates the narrative, Sapphira, and the fact of slavery, the conditions of which emerge for the reader chapter by chapter. Yet, Cather develops the story and marks its passage of time with a constant motif of Easter, of crossing waters at once the Jordan into the Promised Land and the waters of Baptism. In 1856, the time when the action of the novel breaks off and then skips ahead 25 years, who could have told how vastly everything would change? Who could have seen that in the midst of the dying of the miller and his wife and brother, and indeed of the old order of things, new life would come?

Yet, the life of that young slave girl, Nancy, is also more than coincidences. And her return and the presence of her perspective lights the imagination of the little girl who appears in the final chapter who becomes the first person in the story to turn to the unlikely Aunt Till, who tells her "the old stories" until they turn for the first time into "a complete picture" (291-92), presumably the picture Cather has just rendered for us. She, too, from a backwater figured as Jordan, sheds the light that casts away the works of darkness.

It is in such light that we see through what is obscure to what is real, through deceit to truth, through the tangled web to such truth as we are capable of. It is such a light as shined in Paul's prison (in our lesson this morning from Philippians 1:1-11) and allowed him to see not the bars that confined him but love of the people of Philippi that liberated him. And it doesn't matter a bit whether the immediate source of the light is the ragged prophet over the river, a column in the *Red Cloud Chief*, a novel by Willa Cather, or the old, overlooked black slave woman Cather's novel brings into clearer view.

I was e-mailed a little story a month ago. In it, a little boy is telling his Grandma how every single thing seems to be going wrong: at school, at home, with his family, with their health—everything. As Grandma listens, she is baking a cake; and she asks her grandson if he would like a snack. "Sure," he says, brightening just a little. "Well, here," she says, "have a little cooking oil." "Yuck," the boy says. "No?" asks Grandma; "well, how about a couple of raw eggs?" "Grandma," the boy says, "that's gross." "Well, then, how about some baking soda?" "But Grandma," the boy pleads, "those things are all yucky." "Yes," his Grandma replied, "all those things do seem pretty bad all by themselves and just as they are. But they are going to make a delicious cake if only we put them all together the right way and don't leave anything out."

You and I live amidst ingredients, glimpses, fragments; but as Sapphira says to Henry, "these things are beyond us." They are not, however, beyond Him through whom all things came to be and all that is courses toward the complete picture that only the works of darkness now obscure.

VIII

"Keep My Word"

May 18, 2001

Spring Conference

I opened the *Red Cloud Chief* a couple of weeks ago and was delighted to find there the long awaited announcement, "I'm Back!" After some week's sabbatical, Beverley Cooper had returned to writing her column. Her "I'm back" reminded me of things that we lose or that go away and then return, reminded me that what we get back, although identifiable with what went away, is never quite the same. In Miss Cooper's case, the experience of opening the paper and not finding her column has made me appreciate even more than before her humor, insight, and graciousness.

These are wonderful moments, these times when we find again something we'd lost, and find it's even better now. I wonder if we realize how often we wouldn't have had the greater experience if we had not first lost the lesser pleasure.

Of course, the experience I'm referring to isn't always positive. Some of you will remember Freddy of horror picture fame. "I'm back" was his theme, too. And in a way, each time it was the same Freddy. But in a way, each new Freddy was worse than the last. The kernel of much obscured truth in the Freddy series isn't that a man killed over and over can keep turning up, but rather that our pasts can sometimes have a persistent quality of not going away. Sometimes, as Faulkner said, the past isn't history…it isn't even past.

It's funny, isn't it, how most of us have more faith in the return of the bad than in the return of the good?

Something like this background is what we need in order to see how shocking the first line of the scripture from Revelation (21:22-22:5) must have been to its first readers. John opens this passage, his vision of the New Jerusalem, saying, "I saw no temple in the city."

No temple? But as we know from events even today, Jerusalem meant the temple city. For centuries the temple was the heart and soul of Jewish religion. When invaders desecrated the temple in the second century before Christ, the revolt of the Maccabees had as its aim the restoration of the temple, and it is the rededication of the temple that Jews still celebrate at Hanukkah.

Jesus himself was so dedicated to the temple that he put himself in final jeopardy by cleansing it.

How could anyone accept John's vision as authentic when he claims to see the New Jerusalem and in it there is no temple to be seen?

But the truth of what John "sees" is precisely what authenticates his vision, for what he sees is that in the New Jerusalem, "its temple is the Lord God the Almighty and the Lamb." That is, he saw that until people quit worshiping the old temple, they would not be able to begin to worship the new. And notice the order of John's revelation: only when people understood that it was not the temple but what the temple stood for that was important could they find the water of life and the tree of life. And only then would come the time when all understood that "there shall no more be anything accursed." Only then would come the moment when we no longer felt that, to be true to our temple, we had to tear down someone else's, when we no longer had to find those different somehow deficient.

We are hearing how the world's great struggles and pains and conflicts are rooted in how easily we begin to worship the thing, the sign, the place, the tradition instead of what lies behind it. John, too, lived in turbulent times. No wonder he understood how vital it is to see what are the accidents and outward appearances and what is the true essence of one's faith!

Jesus captures this same truth in three simple words in the gospel (John 14:23-29). If anyone loves me, he says, that person will "keep my word." "Keep" is the word of action; "word" is the essence.

And whether it is wat, temple, or church, ashram, synagogue, or congregation, it is the essence of what these buildings or gatherings stand for that counts.

So often Willa Cather captured this in her stories, this attachment to the sign rather than to the significant; she writes of this so often it has begun to strike me as one of the undergirding themes of her literature.

There is of course *The Professor's House*. We enter Godfrey St. Peter's world just at that point when the building of the St Peter's new house has threatened what he holds dear. He resolves not to lose the familiar by keeping his study in the old house, and there he reflects on the comforting images that recall for him the familiar, the old memories. He loves that old house; indeed, he almost loves it to death--his own death. But in the wake of his near death comes the realization that what he had so cherished was really a series of accidents. He comes to know the real thing that transcends location and survives its loss. By the end, he can rejoin the family he is on the way to meet. They will get back the same professor they lost, to be sure; and yet in truth a much different professor, more different Cather tells us than they will know. Only by losing the dear, old house can Godfrey have at least the chance to find himself and become what his name implies.

All this Godfrey could well have learned from his own mentor, Tom Outland; for you will recall that it is not until Tom is dispossessed of the mesa that he can truly possess it, or better, not until he loses it that he can be possessed by it. After Roddy Blake had sold off the artifacts, Tom went back to retrieve his journal; and it was on that trip that he felt as if he were there for the first time, able to see what the mesa had meant.

Perhaps you are already thinking of Bishop Latour in *Death Comes for the Archbishop*. For much of the novel, Latour lives with the grief of the loss of the familiar, the old world in which he was raised. Indeed, his willingness to suffer this loss is his heroism. Then gradually he finds a new object for his attentions: the building of his cathedral. But loss has been a school for Jean Latour, and he proves to be its apt pupil. At some point, possibly in his encounter with the much abused woman to whom he gives his old rosary, he comes to understand that it was neither the old world nor the new, not the seminary nor the cathedral that mattered, but what they point to. Then he can understand how Shiprock is to the Navajo what his Cathedral is to him. Then he can tell us that the two things that really give him joy are the restoration of the Navajo lands and the abolition of slavery. It will not matter whether his body rests in New Mexico or France, for neither New Mexico or France any longer matter.

In *Sapphira and the Slave Girl*, too, the old cherished order must pass before the new can come. Sapphira's house and the social arrangements of which it was the center, these pass. But with Nancy's return we begin to hear the real stories of the lives of the people, the stories once obscured by the very house and history that gave rise to them.

I found myself going on and on through Cather's stories. What John announces in Revelation is everywhere depicted, in the lives of fiddle players to opera singers, sophisticated professors to slave girls. None of this of course makes less the tragedy of our losses, the loss of what our hearts have attached themselves to. But it does make possible the surprise ending, the divine comedy, that just when all is lost, when we find there is no temple in the city, no old house to go on living in, no arrangement of our lives that lasts, no cathedral that is not made of hands—just when we've accepted the reality of our loss, that we discover that the Lord God Almighty was the life in the way of life we cherished, the story in the setting we grew so fond of.

Cather knew her houses and places, loved her church and her history. But, perhaps when the world broke in two, Cather learned that it was not in the blue lake at which Godfrey gazes through his window, but in the dry land of his loss that he would find flowing the water of life. That it was not in the lovely garden where the American mission is planned, nor even in the pale reflections of it that Latour and Vaillant cultivate, but out in the barren desert where they would find the tree of life. And when they have drunk of that water, eaten of that tree, neither the Professor nor the Bishop any longer feel the need to curse those who live or work or play or worship differently than they do.

And when we have drunk of Cather's stories, fed on her remarkable themes, we, too, may just find that, whatever the changes and chances of our mortal lives, we are able to keep not just her words but the word itself, and it may abide in us, whatever its outward manifestations...or ours.

IX

"Lowly Mangers"

December 2001

Cather Birthday Celebration

I set out some time ago to prepare a homily for this special service. You all mean so much to me, and I find myself wanting to do especially well for you, my good companions. But nothing came, and God seemed to be saying to me: wait. I'll inspire you. Trust me.

And so I waited trustingly.

Each time I would return to the matter it would be the same.

The preparations for Thanksgiving went on, but still nothing came. Thanksgiving came and went, but still nothing occurred to inspire me.

Soon, as the season grew closer, Dave Brubeck was playing his renditions of Christmas carols through my stereo speakers, but nothing in them gave me words to say.

Every time I would try to prepare, I would get the same answer: wait, trust.

It was very trying, believe me. It seemed a hard way to be treated. I could recall St. Teresa telling God that he would have more friends if it weren't for the way he treated those he already had.

Day after day the time grew shorter. Still, nada.

Soon it was apparent God was just testing me, testing my trust, belief. He would wait to the last minute, but then on the trip over here, the words would come.

So I settled in for the drive over, knowing, waiting. But nothing. And I began to realize what an embarrassing situation I'd put myself in.

No question now: I was going to have a bad time of it tonight when the time for the homily came. As Red Cloud drew nearer, I began to feel how unfair it was. How could God treat me this way? I didn't deserve it.

That's such an American attitude, don't you think. It is hard for us to be truly grateful to God, not because we haven't received so much, but because so much that we've got we're so sure we've earned, so sure we're entitled to it. That, I suppose, is the down side to our work ethic, our "I can take care of myself" attitude. It doesn't leave much room for that feeling of indebtedness to God that is the meaning of the Jewish Testament's word for thanksgiving, Yadah.

But that isn't important tonight. What's important is what I was thinking as this went on, and what I thought was, well of course you must deserve it, or God wouldn't be treating you this way.

So I began to do what we all do…I asked why me? Why was I undeserving of even the little reward of a few good words for tonight?

And I thought, possibly it is because I'm a Nebraskan. We're kind of a backwater of the world. We don't count for much. Maybe it is because I'm Nebraskan.

It sounds strange when I say that out loud, here, tonight. Yet it didn't seem so strange to feel that way the day after Thanksgiving when we watched the unbelievable on television. Why is it always us? Why is it that the Huskers always break your heart?

And as I sat there that afternoon, there was that other embarrassment of finding myself actually feeling worse than I did on September 11. We can all *say* what means most to us, but real events have a way of giving the lie to what we say.

And it angered me then that God would expose the wretchedness of my heart. How dare he throw such glaring light on how petty my thoughts and sentiments can be. He probably doesn't understand what football means to us, we who have so little else.

We get so used to our little world, don't we? Oh, there's Afghanistan, of course, just as there was Kosovo and before that Somalia and before that Haiti. We know about such things. But that's all television, newspapers. It isn't our world. It isn't the way we think our world is, our little local world that is sometimes all the world to us. Our little prejudices that seem so natural to us. Our little circles, the way we just fall into including some and excluding others. Our little parish of thought and activity and routine.

Well, that's beside the point, isn't it . . . just rambling? No, the point is that there was already that anger for being so let down, that resentment for being so exposed. That was all there, too, through my waiting, my trusting...all there on the way to tonight and . . . this other embarrassment.

Already I did not look good to myself and now I wouldn't look good to you. God hadn't entered my little world and performed the miracle he'd led me to believe would come. The miracle that would change just this one little thing, and of course leave all the rest of my world in tact: my pride, my habits, my work, my standing among my circle of friends. And isn't that kind of miracle we all want: just for that one little change that would leave everything else just the way we are used to it? Just the way we are comfortable?

And as I came to the city limits of Red Cloud, I began to feel very vulnerable. I felt plunged into the growing darkness. As I looked back at the surrounding hills, I wondered where I could find any help that would meet the occasion.

And then came Red Cloud itself, Cather's home, where she had first experienced the lack of sufficient words to explain herself, to make others understand. Where she had come as an outsider, had found those who thought this little world was all the world there was, where she had spent the difficult years of growing up.

And soon, for Red Cloud is small, I was at Grace Church. Now the piper would have to be paid, but there was nothing to do for it. Through the doors into this beautiful rude church, bare bricks and beams and dim light. Perhaps it was my mood, but it seemed not so unlike that stable of the first Christmas, where God emptied himself of all his power and privilege and was born in the vulnerability of a baby, of want, among a people who had not the words to rid themselves of those who held power over them.

And I began to recall how away in that manger God had come into the world. As I tried to focus, the altar here almost seemed for a moment like that manger, and I saw in an instant that when God comes into the world, that world is never the same again. He never just tinkers with one little corner of it and leaves the rest alone. The miracle isn't that one little thing gets taken care of but that the whole thing is made new . . . new and strange and uncomfortable. Nothing looks or feels the same as it did when we were at the center of our little world, because, though he won't enter a room uninvited, when he does enter he becomes the center, his presence fills the room, and all the proportions change. What seemed big in our little world can seem very small indeed; and what seemed small and unimportant becomes something very precious. Our words cease to fill the void as his words echo throughout the room. What was hidden in the secret heart is laid bare, the heart of stone taken away, a new heart given. A new light shines and suddenly our pettiness seems petty, our prejudices seem wrong, our little circle far too narrow and confining.

Something like this must have somehow happened to Cather, too, for her works are full of the self-important cut down to size, the insignificant raised up to unexpected heights, full of the little world lost and the larger, more real world gained.

And just as we were about to begin, I thought I could hear from somewhere the echoing words, "Behold, I make all things new." And all the darkness in which I'd been plunged was cast away and my small, vulnerable self seemed clothed in the armor of God's light.

May it be so for you. Amen.[9]

---

[9] It was not until years after I delivered this sermon that I realized how much it quite possibly owes to having, at one point in time, read a good deal of C. S. Lewis. It is not so much passages, or even ideas, as it is in an outlook one reading Lewis comes

X

"Coats of Many Colors"

May 2002

Spring Conference[10]

Quilts and quilting, the subject of this year's festival, put me in mind of Joseph's many-colored dream coat...not the contemporary play but the ancient coat with its patchwork of fabrics or dyes. At the beginning of the story, the coat is the focus of the brother's jealousy of their seemingly favored brother. They were awfully mean brothers, or he was quite a snot, or the parenting styles were what we would call dysfunctional—something had to be terribly wrong for sibling rivalry to get so out of hand.

Once Joseph is sold into slavery, we hear nothing of the coat again; yet it rules over the rest of the story as a symbol, and often the one thing people remember about Joseph is his coat. By the end of the story, Joseph has himself become the focal point of a strange rescue mission, one of many Israel would look back to in its long history of needing rescue. His story really reaches its climax when he can bring his heart to the thought that what his brothers meant to him for ill, God meant to him for good. This is a spiritual triumph and, standing over it, is the symbol for that triumph, the coat of many colors, and only at this point to we discover what the coat symbolizes.[11]

---

to share. It is not dissimilar to the effect of G. K. Chesterton, or for that matter for any author who gives us a way of looking at things.

[10] The scripture for this homily came from Genesis 37: 1-4, 12-14, 18-20; Psalm 103:8-18; and John 12: 20-26

[11] I am aware that modern biblical scholarship has cast doubt on the translation of the description of Jacob's cloak as a "coat of many colors"—more likely, some say, a coat with long sleeves, denoting someone who didn't need a worker's short sleeves. Possibly so, but a) the difference doesn't affect the way the brothers resent the coat, and b) no writer I know of, certainly neither Cather nor Mann, would have had much reason not to use the text as commonly read.

Years ago, I inadvertently learned something about such symbols in the drawings done in a catechism class by middle schoolers, who, when drawing images that depicted sadness and despair and hurt, drew in monochrome, but when drawing images of forgiveness, hope, and joy, always resorted to the colored pencils.

What others meant to him for ill, God meant to him for good. For Joseph, or for that matter for anyone, this rare thought represents a long spiritual journey, one some never start and many who do never finish. We don't see the idea again in any purity until we see it in the words of forgiveness uttered from the cross.

Now, interestingly enough, Willa Cather wrote a critical piece about Thomas Mann's story, "Joseph and his Brothers." I apologize for belaboring it for those few of you who may be on familiar terms with it but the opening of her review is worth our attending to. Cather wrote that Mann was not trying to capture the "nature of man as the Behaviourists or the biologists see it," but rather presenting humanity in its "double nature, struggling with itself." She went on:

> These ancient people know very little about their physical structure. Their attention is fixed upon something within themselves which they feel to be their real life, consciousness; where it came from and what becomes of it. In this book men ask themselves the questions they asked aeons ago when they found themselves in an unconscious world. From the Old Testament, that greatest record of the orphan soul trying to find its kin somewhere in the universe, and from the cruder superstitions of the neighbouring Semitic peoples, Mann has made something like an orchestral arrangement of all the Semitic religions and philosophies. (*Not Under Forty*, 96-97)

The analogy at the end, this time the analogy of an orchestral arrangement, is like that of quilts where, too, many parts form a greater whole.

It is a long journey from understanding that each person has "a double nature, struggling with itself" to arriving at a willingness not to count men's sins against them. It is the distance between the head and the heart, from knowing what is best to doing what is best.

But, lest we sentimentalize it, that distance will never be traversed if there is nothing in the head to start with, and I'm taken by Cather's understanding of what was in the ancient Hebrew head and heart (the Hebrew wouldn't have distinguished): the orphan soul seeking its kin somewhere in the universe. How often Cather's characters are orphans of one sort or another! What seeking they go through! How they long for a kinship not even so much with another human being but with something true and good and whole beyond ourselves. Each of you can think of some character, a Jim Burden, a Tom Outland, an Ántonia, or a Thea. (Odd, isn't it, how we need the men's whole names but the women's given names are enough).

If we can see that all we human beings have to work with are, as the *Book of Common Prayer* puts it, memory, reason, and skill, then we see immediately how significant a difference it makes what we remember, what kinds of things we have a memory for. Joseph had no memory for what his brothers had done to him, which freed him to reason like God who puts our sins as far from us as east is from west. This, in turn, gave him the skill to rescue Israel. In times or places when we look for those to lead us through crises to new beginnings, we could do worse than to determine what it is our potential leaders have a memory for. Much as we like to compartmentalize, consciousness is not a thing in parts. You can't change our consciousness without changing what we have a mind to remember.

In his article for the recent edition of the *Review*, my friend Joseph Urgo quoted from Cather's "the Best Years" for his epigram:

> The arithmetic teacher "made a joking little talk to the children and told them about a very bright little girl in Scotland who knew nearly a whole play of Shakespeare's by heart, but who wrote in her diary: 'Nine times nine is the Devil'; which proved, she said, that there are two kinds of memory."

Indeed, these two memories are two sensibilities: One insists that justice be done to my coat by insisting that all other coats be like it, while the other has room for the coat of many colors; one insists on the solo part, the other honors the orchestral arrangement; one cherishes the machine-made sheet but the other, the hand-made quilt.

The night before Easter, my wife and I joined some of our Jewish friends in their Passover Seder. The lessons read at the Seder make clear, as does today's news, that we either develop a memory for the grace of God or we surely develop an inability to forget the injustice of the world. A world of walls and tanks or a world of quilts and orchestras and coats of many colors. Joseph first, Cather later—knew on which foundation salvation rests. You cannot read either without encountering encouragement to your own hopes to be faithful to forgiveness.

XI

"Land of Enchantment"

December 6, 2002

Cather Birthday Celebration

Our words this evening from Job are, scholars tell us, among the oldest in the Old Testament.[12] The naming of the constellations was one of the first enterprises of the human race and the words to name them almost as old as human consciousness itself. They form the grammar of wonder, and map the geography of our sense of awe. They place us in a world whose grandeur surpasses human understanding.

And so it was until the Enlightenment, that historical age in which men and women formulated both the democratic ideals of the American Republic and the principles of scientific inquiry. And then the world took a new course, and gradually we began to discover that enlightened thinking reduced the size of the world in which we live. First as science arose, and then as the world began to reject all senses of the world that didn't derive from science, the world shrank.

No doubt it was beneficial to learn that dragons were a figment of the imagination, just as it was to find that disease was actually spread by germs. Hospitals would no longer lay patients on the bedding of the previous patient, women would no longer be burned as witches, and superstition would recede into the background.

At the same time, however, the horizons for each new generation shrank. The sense of life's mystery, life's possibilities gradually

---

[12] Scripture for this Evensong included Job 38:1-33, Psalm 50:1-15, and John 3:1-21. The Rev. Ruth and the late Rev. Larry Jaynes assisted with the service; Nebraska poet Nancy Westerfield read from her poetry. As usual, Barbara Sprague played at the pump organ.

disappeared. The range for the imagination became a matter of fairy tales. Much that had before loomed large in the way people shaped their lives came to be marked FOR CHILDREN ONLY.

We had lost that sense of awe and wonder our remote ancestors had felt when experiencing the changing seasons of the year, when looking up into the sky at night, when weathering the elements, when dreaming of what might be. And generation-by-generation, century-by-century, the suspicion grew that, although the benefits of science and technology were immense, they had not come without a cost. We often had traded for health and progress the human soul, the heart of the matter.

Of course, protests would occasionally arise: the romantic poets struggled to restore the idea of imagination; Thoreau sought to rediscover the transcendent; cults of Shakers and Amish and Hippies took themselves off into isolation away from progress, into reverie and away from activity driven by outcomes. If you are going to San Francisco, be sure to wear flowers in your hair!

In all that history of protest, possibly no single voice spoke more beautifully and surely than that of Willa Cather, and nowhere did she capture both nature and the deprivation of its nurture than in her stunning story, "The Enchanted Bluff."

No stranger to the Land of Enchantment, in more ways than one, Cather sets her story nearby to where we are tonight. Two legs or four wheels are all you would need to get to the site (s-i-t-e), but far more is need to get to the sight (s-i-g-h-t), the insight, the vision in which she invests her scene.

It is in some ways, regardless of the different names she often used for home, the most Red Cloud of all her stories and yet, invested as it is with the distant tale of the Southwest, it is the local made universal. The quite ordinary bluffs nearby become the great bluffs of Southwest and then, in turn, the enchanted bluffs, the vision in which the magic of imagination takes place. And it takes place, just as it always must, just at the moment of crossing the invisible line between childhood and becoming an adult, just at the turning point in the journey to maturity.

There and then the faculty that makes us most truly human is resurrected from the world of progress and development and 2x2 makes 4.[13] For a brief moment what is potential for all lives becomes actual in the lives of her characters, and they dream of actually going to the storied bluffs and set themselves toward their dream. They see what life could be and long for its fulfillment, its mystery, its promise.

It would be a great story had it stopped right there, but it would not have been the whole story, and it would not be Cather's way to tell half a story. As she goes on, it becomes a profound study of the clash of history and the human spirit; for, as she moves on, we find that the dream is never fulfilled. The plan to visit the bluffs, to scale their heights, to abandon the ordinary for the extraordinary becomes, each year that it recedes further from fulfillment, no more than a bluff, an enchanted bluff, players with no cards still raising the ante as though they were still in the game. They are overcome by the world as it is, as it has become, that narrow world of facts; and Cather chronicles the lives of quiet desperation that ensue from forsaking the dream. All but one of them, of course, that one who was leaving for school.

And yet, the story is not finished, the hope not entirely dead, for one of the children of one of the boys has heard the story, has been seized by it as the boys of his parent's generation were. The power of story looms behind the story itself.

Cather, of course, did make the journey, not only to the fabled bluffs of the Southwest, but also through the use to which she put her mind to the land of enchantment itself. It was not **her** courage, not **her** capacity to dream, not **her** feeling for the hopes of men and women and of nations that had failed. And her daring, her virtues, her stories of the human story have left their legacy. Like the child of the new generation in her story, we, too, once children of each of our generations, have heard the story and the spark of imagination has been lit in us. Could we dream big, could we have the courage

---

[13] Of course, closer to our own time, though not outside of the time-frame of Cather's life, developments in all the sciences have, themselves, rejected the purely mechanical and resurrected the mystery, the "quantum."

to pursue the dream, to live as though the dream mattered more than material welfare?

Yet, as we look around us tonight, think: think of the Opera House, the impossible dream. Think of the Willa Cather Pioneer Memorial Foundation [now usually referred to simply as the Cather Foundation] itself, only a dream a few years ago. Think of the festival, and the programs, and the seminars, and the tours, and all that not only passes along the dream but also lives it now. And you who make it all happen—Cather helped to free you from the bonds of the narrow universe in which technology and efficiency would chain us all, and your work stands as a tribute not only to her, not only to story, but to that larger world she helped keep alive, that world shot through with glimpses of the Real Presence and purpose of the Lord.

Over the Opera House, under an inscription of each of your names, should go an inscription: We Are Not Bluffing!

XII

"Glimpses of Grace and Beauty"

December 7, 2003

Cather 130th Birthday Celebration

I have always been struck, like most of you I suppose, by Cather's clothing—the dresses, the jackets, the hats especially. Her fashion statement seems to have been: there are a lot of ugly clothes out there—that doesn't mean I have to wear them.

Yet it has only recently struck me that this may have a larger application to reading Cather, to putting into words something of what we feel we take away from reading one of her works.

When Cather made her now famous remark about the world breaking in two, she was stating an article of faith for the modernist artist. The best-known visual representation of that faith is Picasso's *Guernica* and its portrait of the broken world, helpless against the forces of the century, its ancient symbols of ritual from the bullring in disarray.

"Guernica"

Guernica was prompted by the bombing of a small village as a rehearsal for Hitler's war machine and the painting was a wake up call. Machado would write, "O little Spanish child that comes into the world, may God protect you, for one of the two Spains is bound to freeze your heart." He might as well have said, 'after the world broke in two, one or the other of those worlds will do you in.'

The enemy of the modernist artist was the smug world that couldn't or wouldn't see that there was no hope in the world, that something had radically altered. The enemy was rose-colored glasses, the power of positive thinking, the insistence on a happy ending.

So, if you look at a bit of the history of art and literature you see develop from this period an escalating competition to show just how bad the world really is. Hemingway had captured it in his *A Farewell to Arms*, with Frederick and Catherine escaping a botched war only to suffer through the botched birth of their child, Frederick left at the end to walk home in the rain. Faulkner didn't think Hemingway had gone far enough and in *If I Forget Thee, Jerusalem*, with specific reference to Hemingway, turned that botched birth into a botched abortion, done at the hero's own inept hands. By the time Heller wrote *Catch-22*, he could include the hilarious scene at Thanksgiving in which Lt. Scheisskopf's wife, who, we are told, "didn't believe in God just as much as" Yossarian didn't, but appalled at Yossarian's cynicism, could exclaim that, "the God I don't believe in is a good God, a just God, a merciful God. He's not the mean and stupid God you make Him out to be" (185).

The ironies abound and the horrors grew even worse, first in films such as Sam Peckinpah's *Wild Bunch* and later novels such as Cormac McCarthy's *Blood Meridian* with their portraits of unmitigated brutality. There is always an artist in the wings who believes he or she can show us the horrors of existence better than did those who had come before.

Now, Cather was no stranger to the horrors of existence. The shootings in *O Pioneers*, the mindless cruelty of Ivy Peters slitting the eyes of the little bird, attempted rapes and real abandonment, suicides…all these abound in her work, the saddest of which, to my mind, is the tragic story of *My Mortal Enemy* based in the life of the

McClures. And yet, it has been my experience and that of countless readers that these horrors are not the lasting impression left by any of her works. Despite their unflinching gaze at the realities of the world, we come away with something else, with glimpses of grace and beauty.

I was reminded of this in the recent mailings of the Cather Foundation promoting their line of Christmas cards and the raising of the matching funds. (Incidentally, I hope you have already bought yours. I'm a shameless moneychanger in the temple and don't mind at all hawking those cards or that cause from the pulpit, however sure it is to bring down someday the scourge!) If you've received these, you know they feature the scene from *My Ántonia* of Jim's family and their hired men decorating the Christmas tree in homespun style. This is how the passage reads:

> The cedar was about five feet high and very shapely. We hung it with the gingerbread animals, strings of popcorn, and bits of candle…. Its real splendours, however, came from the most unlikely place in the world—from Otto's cowboy trunk…. There was the bleeding heart, in tufts of paper lace; there were the three kings, gorgeously apparelled, and the ox and the ass and the shepherds; there was the Baby in the manger, and a group of angels, singing; there were camels and leopards, held by the black slaves of the three kings. Our tree became the talking tree of the fairy tale; legends and stories nestled like birds in its branches. (54-55)

I'm not sure what that leopard is doing there, but then I keep a lobster tail in our crèche, so who am I to judge. Of course, leopard or lobster, they remind us that the manger scene is just a microcosm; but our lobster is there mostly to remind us there are people in Maine who have done us many kindnesses.

This contrast, the contrast between the world broken in two, not unlike the host at a Eucharist, and the joy surrounding that tree, were on my mind when I came to look at the lessons for this Sunday (the

2nd Sunday of Advent in the liturgical churches). This is what we read earlier from Baruch:[14]

> Take off the garment of your sorrow and affliction, O Jerusalem, and put on forever the beauty of the glory from God.

This seems what Cather was able to do not only in how she dressed but also in how she wrote. Of course the world is full of sorrow and affliction. The birth of Christ, an old hymn tells us, takes place in the bleak midwinter, and no one could capture bleak midwinter better than Cather. You will recall her passage:

> Winter lies too long in country towns; hangs on until it is stale and shabby, old and sullen…the scene of human life…spread out shrunken and pinched. (*MA* 116)

Oh, she could capture the bleak world all right. But she could look away from the world long enough to see the glimpses of truth, beauty, and goodness, glimpses that she shares with us. There were plenty of ugly clothes in the world, but she didn't need to wear them. She didn't need to make a perpetual raiment of the world's sorrows and afflictions.

I can picture her in New York's Ascension Church, looking at the La Farge mural of the Ascension, and putting on forever the beauty of the glory from God. I can picture her doing that right here in the country church where we are gathered tonight. Looking away from this world, she could know the joy of the other, could walk in the light of a glory not of this world but real all the same, could picture, for herself and for us, the mercy and righteousness that come from God. She knew how to read the world through the eyes of eternity.

My mother, Dot Peek, had her favorite seasonal verses. The one for this season went like this:

---

[14] The scriptures for the homily came from Baruch 5:1-9, Psalm 126, and Luke 3:1-6, the lessons for Advent 2 C

Christmas is coming;
The geese are getting fat.
Pray put a penny
In a poor man's hat.
If you haven't got a penny,
A ha'penny will do;
And if you haven't got a ha'penny,
Then God bless you.

You know—Christmas is not good news for the goose!

Nothing is good news to everybody, and especially if you see yourself as the goose about to be cooked.

But what good news the season has always been to the poor and the poor in spirit, who receive the promise to see God. What good news it was to those cast out by the political and religious authorities of Jesus' day: the lepers, the beggars, the women, the children, the seekers after truth. Good news to those who could take off the garment of sorrow and affliction and put on forever the beauty of the glory from God.

I suspect, you see, that what we take away from a Cather book is not her Christmas stories, but the Christmas story, the sense that something has occurred in our world that changes forever how we see it and gives us hope.

In that spirit I want to close with the Christmas reflection and prayer of another Cather fan: Frank Griswold, Presiding Bishop of the Episcopal Church:[15]

> The piercing wail of a newborn child shatters the silence of the night, and the peace of God which passes all understanding is unleashed upon a

---

[15] The Rt. Rev. Frank Griswold not only served as Presiding Bishop of the Episcopal Church, but also wrote some of the 1979 *Book of Common Prayer*; he is an avid reader of Cather and would give an excellent keynote address to a subsequent Spring Conference.

broken world. May that same peace be born in us and show forth in our lives, giving hope to those without hope and overcoming the hostilities that divide us one from another. Let us rejoice and welcome Christ, who is the morning star rising in our hearts and giving to the world the light of his deathless and all embracing love. Amen.

XIII

"The Risk of Living"

May 1, 2004

Spring Conference

People of the Christian faith are often called "an Easter people," and often that is taken to mean they hold a certain belief about the Resurrection of Jesus Christ.

I don't doubt for a moment that this is true as far as it goes. St. Paul tells us that if Christ has not been raised, then our faith is in vain. The church is not meant to be a museum for preserving the memory of a dead Lord.

I am doubtful, however, that a statement, a creed of belief about an event is really what it means to be an Easter people. I'm doubtful, first of all, because in my life I've met or heard about folks who seemed like Easter people, some of whom didn't share the Christian faith. And I'm doubtful, secondly, because being an Easter people seems to me to imply something more about how we live than just what we believe.

Here we are at a festival one of whose special topics is aging and, in Jo Ann Middleton's words from last night, about the "fearsome threshold of death," and at the same time we are here looking at the "last things," the church is in the midst of her Easter celebration. On both counts, then, it seemed to me appropriate to take us back to a scene that I revisit often, the scene of the resurrection, which is after all a tomb. It is one of those scenes that bears out, perhaps more than any other scene for us in the Western World, the truth of what that great chronicler of the world's stories, Joseph Campbell, calls the mono-myth. According to Campbell, we share two experiences. The first is that we become well aware that in the midst of life there is death. At my age, that awareness is pressed upon me more and more often, and as many of you know, was pressed on me with some sharpness in my own recent confrontation with mortality. But the second experience, an epiphany of sorts, is that in the midst of death there is life.

The scene of the Christian story of the resurrection is so like Cather's scenes: a symbolic landscape that evokes feelings we can't quite put our finger on. Surely, the story is meant to put us in mind that even in the midst of death there is life. What sort of people are we, what manner of living do we grow into, if we sense that there is life even in death? The answer to that hangs on the few, mysterious, striking details of the story of the resurrection.[16]

First of all, the women arrive at the tomb to anoint the body. They do so at no little peril either to themselves or to their reputations. If they are the first Easter people, then being an Easter people means being willing to accept risk. Note that I used the phrase accept risk, not just take risks…any fool and many teenagers take risks every day…most people will do it if the reward is great enough, and some thrive on the adrenalin flow of taking risks. But these women had nothing to gain. They weren't thrill seekers, breaking up the boredom of their lives with an adventure. They were people willing to accept risk, to not let their behavior be determined by their fears.

At a church I served, we had started up a "lunch bunch," a once a month lunch for seniors over 75. One day, sitting around a table, one of them announced that she had the opportunity to go to China. She was in her 80s and obviously such a trip presented certain hazards. One of her friends said, Helen, you must go. Never give in to your fears. Those folks were an Easter people.

The women arrive and find the stone rolled away from the tomb. That stone has always been to me the central symbol in the story. It seems to me the accumulated weight of all that we find hard to let go of, to get rid of, the stuff that seems immoveable, the baggage that weighs us down but we somehow convince ourselves is

---

[16] The scripture for this homily was drawn from Revelation 7:9-17 and John 10:22-30

necessary for our trip. I once sponsored a young man in a twelve-step program. He was a troubled fellow, but for a while seemed to make progress. His real problem was that he was afraid of responsibility and a technicality that had made him eligible for vocational rehabilitation kept him from the necessity of work. He could never give up the security of that vocational rehabilitation grant. He couldn't roll away that stone. He couldn't muster the idea that behind it was new life waiting. And ultimately he went back to his old ways. He was a professed Christian, but he wasn't, for all that, one of the Easter people. Easter people can let go.

So the witnesses enter and find the empty shroud. That empty shroud is so intangible, isn't it? It is provocative but proves nothing. It is merely linen cloths but it means so much more to them. Many a youngster has been captivated by intangible goals, only to have a pragmatic elder belittle the goals simply because they were intangible. Recently, as you may know from the news, a young woman from a prestigious law firm, took a leave to go to Africa to investigate the claims of abuse by women held in refugee and prison camps. She became so taken with the project that when she returned, she resigned and went to Iraq to promote women's equality in the coming nation. There was nothing in it for her, the dream so intangible next to the solid status and income of her law practice, her death by gunshot so real. And I do not know what her faith was or if she had belonged to any organized church or religion. But I do know she was one of the Easter people. She had seem the empty shroud, the intangible significance, and lived in pursuit of it.

Then, just as ephemeral, a figure appears who tells the women, the witnesses to go. And they go. They are people with a mission. Their life revolves around a sense of purpose that gives meaning to every occasion, every activity. Easter people do not just grimly hang on, conserve, preserve. Everything seems to them changed, the whole creation new; they live in a world of possibilities. An Easter people know serenity and purpose and resolve.

If in youth, part of our life is to become acquainted with the world, then in maturing it is part of our life to become acquainted with what is out of this world, what transcends our places and times and moments. Older age looms ahead as either a time of bitterness, of cynicism, or as a time of hope and contentment. Paul Olson, in the title of one of his later books, called such growth a journey to wisdom. The symbols of that wisdom are what foreground the story of the empty tomb.

It has always seemed to me that Cather, herself, belonged to that company of Easter people. She knew what it was like to have her world break in two, but she accepted that as the risk of living. At each stage of her life and her writing, she rolled away the stone of past success, of previous styles and structures, and moved on to something new. She felt her art as a calling, a vocation, a mission; and in the purpose of that life she found serenity and meaning.

She must have, or how else would she have conceived of that exemplar of Easter people in all places and times, Neighbor Rosicky? Moving from the string of defeats that are recounted in retrospect, he throws off the clinging weight of the past and embraces a new future. Accepting the risk of farming, he celebrates when drought takes his crop. He closes his life on a mission, a mission especially for Polly, and he ends his life in the serenity of the village cemetery, his epitaph spoken by his doctor.

Not particularly religious, indeed mocking of some of religion's strictures and postures, he nevertheless knows not only that death is found in the midst of life, but also that life is found in the midst of death. He may have no orthodox creed, or any creed at all, but he knows the force that makes all things new, and knowing it, he lives in the light of it. I owe him and his creator a debt of thanks, for Rosicky's example helped me recently to practice what I preach.

There in his story, as well as in the life of his creator, we find all the human and emotional artifacts of the empty tomb: the peril and the risk, the letting go, the embrace of those intangibles that give us strength and purpose. Rosicky and the artist who invented him put us all closer to that intangible but vibrant life that lies behind the stone, that life that, if we have the courage to risk it, lives even in the midst of dying.

XIV

"Dreams in the Wilderness"

June 3, 2006

Spring Conference

The three great Christian Feasts are all borrowed, and in good Cather fashion they were all borrowed pretty eclectically. The Christian celebration of Christmas piggy-backed itself on a Norse festival, which is why Christmas was added later in the Christian calendar—Christianity didn't reach northern Europe until later in its history. Easter piggy-backed on spring festivals Christianity found in the Greco-Roman world in which it made its start. And Pentecost was borrowed from the calendar of the Jews among whom Christianity first arose.

This business of borrowing originated out of a desire to honor the truths found in the religious beliefs Christianity encountered, add to them the truth Christianity preached, and start an open dialogue between Christianity and pagan religions. This began in St. Paul's apparent belief that, though Christianity possessed the truth, it did not possess all truths; and this idea is expressed in our own times most notably by C. S. Lewis and J. R. R. Tolkien, whose Narnia and Shire are currently all the rage.

The term Christian writer rests easily on Lewis or Tolkien, but in its wider meaning it could easily rest on Cather as well. I would call her a Christian writer in the sense that she often drew ideas and images from the Christian tradition and set those ideas and images in the context of first encounters with people of other beliefs in places with different histories. Centuries of Christian supremacy may have blurred the vision of this more primitive Christian tradition, but it is to this tradition Cather most obviously belongs, as we can see most notably in *Death Comes for the Archbishop*, but to no small degree in *My Ántonia* and most assuredly in *Shadows on the Rock* as well.

Now the lessons we heard read today are those from the Revised Common Lectionary for the celebration of Pentecost, that singular event with various biblical portraits, in which the Apostolic community received, amidst images of rushing wind and tongues of fire, the promised gift of the Holy Spirit and, infused by this spirit, began, as one part of the text says, "to speak in other tongues," or, as another part of the text reads, to speak in such a way that "each one heard them speaking in his own language" (Acts 2: 4, 6).[17]

In a traditional way and setting, one might celebrate the Pentecost event, as some do, in a ritual of red vestments and hangings that recall the tongues of fire in the upper room. Or, in a more radical way, one might celebrate the Pentecost event, as yet others do, by cultivating glossolalia (the speaking in tongues). But one might, also, less traditionally but perhaps more truly celebrate Pentecost by taking note of how the early Christian community found in the event the possibility of a new heart, a new mind, a new understanding.

In the reading from Acts, the author, Luke, hearkens back to the Jewish prophet Joel and Joel's sense that, when the spirit of God would finally come, it would not so much place us in the right pew in the right church as it would inspire the human imagination. As Joel put it, the people would prophesy, they would have visions, they would dream dreams. Paul boils that dreaming down to its simplest form: people would find a way to hope for that which they didn't and couldn't see. And finally, in the gospel of John, we are told that the Spirit of God, when it comes upon us, will lead us into all truth.

These readings would have been marvelously suggestive for someone of Cather's artistic temperament and creative process. She would have noted how these readings showed Jews encountering Jesus speaking first to other Jews and then to those who were

---

[17] The scripture for this homily was taken from Acts 2:1-21, Psalm 105:25-35, 37b; Romans 8:22-27; and John 15:26-27 and 16:4b-15

neighbors of the Jews in the ancient world. She would have noted how those writers were striving to portray for the listener or reader the fulfillment of the most fundamental and universal and heartfelt of human hopes. And she would have shared in the identification of that hope as just this: that, though at any given moment we don't know the whole truth, there is a spirit that, once embraced, can lead us there.

Nor would Cather have neglected the meaning of the historical developments from those biblical times to the times in which she set her stories. She would have known that later Christians would make the claim, not entirely unjustified (although a bit neglectful of the powerful role that Islam played in the process), that the seeds planted at Pentecost were what grew into the later flowering of civilization, the hope heralded by Paul feeding the rise of the belief in Progress, the powers of the imagination in Luke's account feeding the rise of the Arts, and the Truth championed by John becoming the foundation for the rise of Higher Learning.

Of course, this development from seed to flower did not happen over night. It took centuries before the great arts of Europe began to be seen, but then far fewer centuries before the rise of Romanticism came out of and affected those arts, and then even less time before the dawn of the "religion of art," art that would not so much mean as be. That exponential quickening, that rapidly quickening motion of time, was largely the result of the age of exploration and conquest, during which the values of the old world were challenged by the conditions of the new, and the new world presented itself to the European mind as the New Eden on which humanity could make a new beginning.

Shadows on the Rock represents this broad yet biblical way of understanding Pentecost, understanding it as the possibility of coming to the kind of mind that can be led into new truth; and in this novel, Cather portrays people of just this kind of heart and mind, catching them in the act so to speak, seeing her characters' acts as the latter day acts of latter day apostles.

With this background, one can begin to see that *Shadows on the Rock* is, albeit loosely, a Pentecost novel. In it Cather acknowledges the value of those who, unlike their fellows, possess a mind that is open to change, open to new truth; and she creates a scene in which the imaginations of those touched by the Spirit can see visions and dream dreams.

The Auclairs and other settlers arrive in the New World having traversed an ocean, a passage that did not just weaken but obliterated the ties with the Old. We find Madame Auclair, with the others, perched out on "this rock in the wilderness," dreaming a dream for Cecile, thinking "how much she was entrusting to that little shingled head; something so precious, so intangible; a feeling about life that had come down to her through so many centuries and that she had brought with her across the wastes of brutal, obliterating ocean. The sense of 'our way,'—that was what she longed to leave with her daughter" (20).

What Madame Auclair senses early in the novel is affirmed toward its end, when the Bishop tells Monsieur Auclair, "the old age is dying, but the new is still hidden" (227). Faced with this reality, even the missionaries have suffered "an almost continuous sense of the withdrawal of God" (123). In the midst of the trauma of change, the settlers feel both the need and the possibility to wed "the good manners of the Old World, the dash and daring of the New," as they are found together in Pierre Charron (p. 139).

Into the spiritual geography of the settlement on the rock, Cather as usual weaves the frontier of the mind. Although he thinks, "He was not of the proper stuff for a colonist," Euclide Auclair lives up to his auspicious name (Euclidian clarity) by possessing the "lively and inquiring spirit" of one whose "thoughts were pictures" (6). And, Cather notes, "Although he was so content with familiar scenes and faces as to be almost afraid of new ones, he was not afraid of new ideas, —or of old ideas that had gone out of fashion" (23). How remarkable, even today: someone who judges ideas by their truth, not by whether they are new or old!

Similarly, the courageous Ursulines and Hospitalières, "had no hours of nostalgia, for they were quite as near the realities of their lives in Quebec as in Dieppe or Tours. They were still in their accustomed place in the world of the mind (which for each of us is the only world)." For them the drama "went on in Quebec just as at home" and for them, too, "there was always hope" (78).

Though these settlers may have landed on a rock in the wilderness, their challenge is the frontier everyone faces, the frontier of Everyman, or as *Shadows on the Rock* would ultimately have it, Everywoman: to have such spiritual properties of mind and heart as produced "the little shades of feeling which make the common fine" (21).

Cather comes toward the conclusion of *Shadows on the Rock* with an emblem like the one she employs in "Two Friends," this time with Hector Saint-Cyr, the priest, recalling:

> Certain naked islands in the Gulf of St. Lawrence; mere ledges of rock standing up a little out of the sea, where the sea birds came every year to lay their eggs and rear their young in the caves and hollows; where they screamed and flocked together and made a clamour, while the winds howled around them, and the spray beat over them. This headland was scarcely more than that; a crag where for some reason human beings built themselves nests in the rock, and held fast. 182

In Cather's gloss, the rock may be shadowed by ages of tumults of change, but standing on it, though "entirely cut off" from our history and in "severance from the world," we can still glimpse, among the ships that come and go, *La Bonne Espérance*—the good hope (6). That would seem a Pentecost worth keeping. And it is, I believe, the Pentecost that Cather (who usually understood and felt more than most of us) kept in her heart and mind and wrote in *Shadows on the Rock*.

XV

"Where the Sacred Is Made Known"

Spring 2007

Spring Conference

Our time is short today, so I will be brief . . . and I know you are thinking, well, we'll see how that actually works out!

When I was young, sci-fi movies began to come into their own. Flying saucers would visit earth, bringing aliens to our planet. I was particularly fascinated by those aliens who were a vaguely human-shaped blob: featureless, expressionless, even motionless. They were a sort of pure being; like God as God is pictured at the beginning of Genesis, they merely thought and then something happened without any intervening mechanism.

That seemed alien to me indeed. To shoot someone down playing cowboys and Indians, I needed a pistol. To get somewhere, I needed a bike. These aliens needed, well, nothing. No thing!

How different that world is from the scriptures whose actors are surrounded by material and physical objects, objects that often play a crucial role.

In the Old Testament lesson I chose for this morning, it is Elijah's spirit that Elisha wants, but he gets it through taking the cloak Elijah leaves behind. He puts on Elijah's mantle and through this gains Elijah's spirit.[18]

---

[18]

The scripture for this homily was drawn from 2 Kings 2: 1, 8-14; Psalm 92: 1-9; and John 9:1-7. The theme of the conference was "material culture."

In one of the more memorable healings in the New Testament, that of Blind Bartimaeus, the description in the Gospel of Mark goes out of its way to tell us that, before coming to Jesus, Bartimaeus threw off his mantle, his cloak. The cloak or mantle, the material object, had to be put off before he could put on Christ and his gift of sight. Clearly Mark had in mind Elisha, taking off his own cloak and tearing it in two before he put on Elijah's.

In the gospel reading I chose for today from John, Jesus uses his spit to make a clay poultice to put over the blind eyes and tells the man to go immerse himself in the pool of Siloam. In the act we will commemorate today, Jesus took bread, took the cup.

All these mantles and poultices and pools and cups—all these physical and material objects—puzzle me in just the opposite way from what bothered me with the aliens from outer space. If Jesus wanted to heal, why didn't he just think: be healed? If Elijah's spirit is to pass on to Elisha, why doesn't it just pass, invisible, unseen, immaterial? If Christ wanted his mystical presence to remain with his followers, why the table, why the plate, why the cup?

Yet both the older and newer testaments insist that spiritual realities be tied to and make use of material realities; there is always reference to and use of the most elementary of the objects of our material culture: the clothes we wear, the vessels from which we eat.

And through this the scriptures announce what is sometimes called the sacramental principle. Sacraments we are told are outward and visible signs of inward and invisible graces. We are tied to, immersed in our material culture; in Christianity, God, to come to us through that culture, comes by way of those material objects. To be present with us, to be incarnate, God became human, not in some pretend way, but in the real way, in the way of physical beings surrounded by and dependent on the materials of our existence.

I recall a story once that I heard as boy in Colorado. A Texan was visiting Colorado, and his host was trying to impress him with its grandeur. He showed him the Rockies, the tumbling rivers, the snow caps, the deep gorges, the trees and timberlines. After a bit, the Texan said, I'll admit those are pretty impressive, but take away the mountains and rivers and vistas—and what have you got? That's easy, said his host. You've got Texas. (My apologies to the Texans among us—perhaps the storyteller had never been to the Hill Country!)

It won't do to over spiritualize Christianity. Perhaps the bread and wine, cups and plates, mantles and poultices are impressive bits of theater. But what you've got of the Christian story when you take them away—is nothing.

Gathering here this morning, we all know how keenly Cather understood the significance of the objects of our material and physical culture. Our conference will be spent in enumerating examples of how Cather rendered the material world in her fiction and to what effect, so I won't take our time this morning to do so. However, with this theme of material culture and this sacramental principle in mind, I think especially of Thea Kronberg and Cather's emphasis in her depiction of her physicality. On stage, she begins to become conscious, in Cather's words, "that her body was absolutely the instrument of her idea" (478). In language Steve Shively reminds us echoes that of the Eucharist, Cather tells us that Thea "had begun to understand that—with her at least—voice was, first of all vitality; a lightness in the body and a driving power in the blood" (307). Unlike the aliens of my childhood films, Thea does not just think music—she makes music. And making music requires vocal chords and pianos and stages.

And why should we—many not Episcopalians, some not Christians, and in any event here for a conference, not for Church—why should we gather here at Grace Church as part of our day? Why not just think about its theme? Why gather in a place and among the material objects of that place? Because it is a place, and these are among the objects that correlate us with our quest for a share in Cather's spirit. Because places and the things that go with them are important to us and, therefore, important to God.

Expressing how she came to be churched, the Rev. Deacon Eyleen Farmeer wrote,

> At first, I sat through liturgies that were unfamiliar, tried to sing hymns that I didn't know, and filed haltingly up to the communion rail to receive the bread and wine. I didn't realize I was falling in love. But gradually, over the course of a couple of years, I began to recognize what was happening. I was being beckoned—perhaps even wooed—into a deeper life with God. And sometimes the music really is so beautiful it takes my breath away. And sometimes, as I press bread into the small, sweaty hands of a child, or into the knotted, arthritic hands of the aged, I get tears in my eyes. Sometimes the stained glass windows, the flowers, the vestments, the candles come together in such a way that I really am in a different—a sacred—place. ("In Another Place," *The Anglican Digest* Lent AD 2007)

Bishop John Bryson Chane of the National Cathedral says something quite similar:

> We celebrate this Cathedral as the place where the sacred is made known to us through art, architecture, music, prayers, and the incarnational presence of God as revealed in the Eucharist. The stones that mark the outward presence of this Cathedral also mark the inward and mystical presence of God. We are surrounded by living stones, shaped by human hands to help define what is so hard to know. God is among us, demanding the best we have to offer to God and to the world and all who inhabit it. ("For the Emerging Generation," *Cathedral Age* Winter 2007, 30)

How fitting, then, if we would know God, or even if we would simply know Cather, that we attend today, as the theme of the conference directs us, to the mantles and cups, the poultices and pools, the material culture. It is our only culture, the medium through which all other significant and spiritual realities come to us, enter our lives, open our eyes, and make us human.

That is unless, of course, we are aliens.

XVI

"Feeding the Hungry"

June 2010

Spring Conference

Long before this spring conference on food and wine, the Jesus Foundation had what some say was its first conference, also on food and wine; it was called the Last Supper. And as those gathered listened to the speaker on that occasion, what he said to them about bread and wine resonated with so many of the themes of manna in the wilderness, water from the rock, and feedings of 5000; and it reminded them of how the Hebrew Testament is full of recipes of what they could and could not eat and how it was and was not to be prepared.[19]

They couldn't have failed to recall how Jesus had focused those themes in his parable in Matthew 13:33: The kingdom of heaven is like leaven that a woman hid in three measures of flower until it was all leavened.

There would have been for that audience, Jewish, mind you, not Christian, three "aha" moments in the biblical echoes they heard.

The first would have been surprise that the kingdom could be like leaven—since the chief Jewish feast celebrated the Exodus and its unleavened bread. They may well have had what we would call a "depression mentality"—that is, they may well have been locked into

---

[19] The scripture for this homily was drawn from Genesis 18:1-10a; Psalm: 148; and Matthew 13:33. I'm indebted here to Barbara Brown Taylor and what she often draws from the parables of Jesus and to Kenneth Bailey and the perspective of Middle Eastern culture he brings to reading the parables.

a previous time of desperation and shortage rather than looking toward the security of blessings to come. Here, however, was the rabbi addressing how we have to take the last of the old harvest while a future harvest is yet to come, have to live out of a faith and a hope.

Second, as we heard read, they would have recognized the Old Testament "type" for this business of measuring meal. Their memories would have gone to Abraham and Sarah, who, upon seeing three strangers, immediately set about preparing a meal with "three measures" of flour. Now there is an element of "Measure" humor here—a measure is somewhere around 50-60 pounds . . . so Abraham and Sarah are portrayed as preparing for something unknown but bound to be momentous!

They would, I think, have made another connection. As Greeks often conceived of Woman as being like a field, so the Jews often saw Woman as like an oven. And this means, they would have made a connection in their minds between cooking bread and "incubating" a child. That is, it would not have surprised them that these meal preparations and their directions were not particularly about cooking!

In that context, it comes as no surprise that the hospitality shown by Abraham and Sarah is a preface for the strangers' announcement that the barren Sarah will give birth, and give birth not just to a child but to a lineage, a faith, a people, a people of word who congregated around men of words, the rabbis, to hear God's word, to be taught God's ways.

And this leads us to another important connection of symbol (see again Mark 8:15). Upon hearing "leaven," Jesus' audience would have thought of "teaching." Jesus would often phrase a warning about the Pharisees' teaching by calling on his listeners to "beware of the leaven" of the Pharisees.

This has one further ramification. While in the pharisaic teaching—of Jesus's time or our own—it is completely all right for woman to be a cook . . . but another matter for her to be cooking up a lesson, that is for the figure of the cook to be a figure for teaching. I can imagine some in earshot of Jesus saying, "A woman rabbi?"

So let us unpack what the parable tells us the Kingdom of God is like. It is like this: It's like people who don't bring their teaspoon or cup but their sack, their barrel. It's the blessing on they who go overboard! Who are passionate. It is like people who reach out with all they've got to do something good and great. It is like people who don't get stuck in the hard times but look toward blessing. Who get ready for good things, for receiving blessings, for ways of being blessings.

The kingdom involves being open to change, to new roles, and embracing them with gusto! Steve Shively reminded us of the kinds of hunger and hungering Cather chronicles—the kingdom is where these hungers are addressed and met.

In their minds and hearts they would have heard again all the connections we know but somehow always find hard to believe: connections between hearth and heart. They would have noted the very connection of which David Porter reminded us last evening, the connection of nature and culture, of community and economics, and of which Sue Maher reminded us yesterday, the connection of soil and soul.

And in those connections they would have come, again or for the first time, to the realization that bread and belief are mutual elements of life—more than just our bellies hunger and we live not by bread alone. These are the connections Cather often saw and rendered, drawing us to foods and tables where bodies, minds, and spirits could be fed.

XVII

"Figuratively Speaking"

June 2012

Spring Conference

In the May 2012 edition of *Prairie Fire: the Progressive Voice of the Great Plains*, Bob Thacker wrote (and I excerpt):

> In the years following Willa Cather's death in April 1947, some of her friends and admirers remarked on the meaning and significance of her first book, "April Twilights," a slim volume of poems that had been published in early 1903 by Richard G. Badger in Boston . . . the firm had also published Edward Arlington Robinson's first book, and Cather's, though largely ignored once her fiction had made her reputation, managed a review in the New York Times. Looking back at her friend's early career from about 1950, the playwright and poet Zöe Akins saw Cather's beginnings as poet as crucial to the distinctive, clear prose she later produced in her fiction . . . Dorothy Canfield Fisher . . . argued that Cather was throughout her life possessed of a poet's sensibility, one that is felt throughout her fiction.
> http://www.prairiefirenewspaper.com/comment/reply/1392 - comment-form

It makes one wonder why we have waited so long to celebrate Cather's poetry! The idea arose even before I was President of the Board of Governors and I want to thank Steve Shively, the first person I heard mention this idea, and Bob Thacker, our conference organizer, for seeing the idea become a reality.

In honor, then, of the conference's long-awaited exploration of Cather's poetry, I want to start with a little poem of my own, hoping it won't desecrate the sublime occasion:

Faulkner and Cather both saw themselves as poets, failed I suppose,
And so fortunately for us forced to turn to prose,
There to portray lost causes and a lost lady or two,
Enough to convey new worlds to readers, even today, until you
Find yourself drawn into their worlds, worlds without rhyme,
But which, in poetry, reveal their reason across the great abyss of time;
Both, like Whitman, shameful at the work of self promotion,
Yet neither, Bill nor Willa, took well to all the fuss and commotion
That comes with success, wishing at times they could shift into reverse
And find themselves back in that room of their own, filled simply with verse.

Facts can be stated (as they routinely are on your medicine bottle) but we moderns have been slow to learn that even the concept "fact" is relatively new and, therefore, not particularly a definitive guide to goodness, truth, or beauty.

Great voices from the 20th century—contemporaries of Cather—have raised one common theme: that truth, unlike facts, cannot be directly stated. Indeed, while Wittgenstein traced this notion clear back to Socrates, it was not what I might call the "common witness" until the modernists in literature and the language philosophers following Wittgenstein.

To try to state truth as simply facts or formulas is always fatuous.

The implication of this seemed clear to the bright new minds of the late 19th and early 20th centuries. Truth can only be stated figuratively, that is as poetry, as metaphor.

This Cather well knew who knew how something, even something as important as the past, was—for all its significance—simply incommunicable.

There was indeed something if not religious at least truly spiritual to this idea and, as we know, to Cather's life, ideas, and language. I think many would readily agree with that if I posed it instead as a rhetorical question: "To how much poetry does the poetry of the Garden of Eden and the Garden of Gethsemane seem to have given rise?"

The New Testament is nothing if not a figure of speech, and in that it shares with the Jewish Testament usually attached to it, the Quran (usually and unfortunately not even associated with it), the Upanishads, or any other book that presents what its believers hold to be scripture, that is hold to be sacred words, words that help us get to the bottom of things.

The building blocks of religion are either towers to storm the heights and be like God (cf. the Tower of Babel) or metaphors to plumb the depths and be, finally, human.

Eventually, the towers all come tumbling down (though often not until they've done much harm). If tangible powers, such as towers and tanks, are more prevalent, it is because they are much easier to build. Metaphors are harder to construct, to construe, to conceive— each a virgin birth of sorts, at once original, yet universal.

Think for a moment how scripture is poetry.

My apologies to the late Jerry Falwell, but in the Hebrew scriptures there were the obviously poetic books, such as Genesis and its creation stories, legends, and sagas; there were the books of prophetic visions; there were the psalms and laments. String those together with some genealogies, usually more fiction than poetry, and you have the older of the two scriptures that we count as the Judeo- Christian tradition.

The Christian scriptures run the gamut from the great similes of St. Paul (if I speak with the tongue of men or of angels, and have not charity, I am a tinkling cymbal, a sounding gong) to Jesus' not last but first resort: metaphor (I am the vine, you are the branches); and from there to the two most vivid examples of poetics, the parables of Jesus and the vision of the Beloved Disciple.

Much that is amiss today comes from the mischief of trying to make facts of these poetic discourses!

Given what they convey, they could be nothing other than poetry. How else would you express the mystery that the divine is present in the midst of disaster and death except by sweeping a hand over a dinner table and calling its food and drink your body and blood? How else reach dull ears except to wash their feet? "Sir," some Greeks tell Phillip, "we would see Jesus." "A grain of corn must fall into the earth and die before it can bring forth fruit," they are told. A desperate longing for something to hang onto is met with a metaphor!

Cather was not, of course, the first writer to know her scripture, to find in its preference for poetry a spur to one's own, to create in one's artistry the sense that the truth can be beheld but not described, to come by the desire to paint a word picture, like the picture of Daniel in the Lion's Den, like Isaiah's description of the suffering servant, like the story of a woman caught in adultery, like the understanding of our relationship to God in the metaphor of the marriage feast of the lamb.

And Cather was not the last artist for whom the poetry of scripture was a shaping influence. Think of Bill Kloefkorn and how what he heard in Church as a boy gave him the biblical cadences of his work. Think of Charles Fort and how an American Baptist background influenced his keen sense of metaphor.

Cather knew her scripture directly, of course; but she would have known it indirectly as it was filtered through the Baptist hymnal and the Episcopal *Book of Common Prayer* and the Angelus and other devotions of the Roman Catholic missions. It would be hard to ignore the shaping influence that these, taken together, had on her work, in both its poetry and its practice.

The poetry of the Church gave her a platform from which to plunge into Panther Canyon, a blueprint for the spiritual architecture of the Professor's house, an Angelus to ring at the death of an Archbishop, a tradition by which to transubstantiate the experience of her childhood and later life into enduring art, a spiritual biology for giving birth to beauty.

Having, then, begun with my doggerel, let me end, as a tribute to Cather's poetry and poetics and to the conference of that theme, with a poem of Charles Fort's and allow that poem to join our prayers and hymns and lift us from the prosaic into the powerful poetry that shapes and defines us all:[20]

"For Two Daughters"
For Claire and Shelley

There is no history in their eyes
as they tap the lilac drum and birch,
roll out the silver necklace into a straight line
over the stone and open wound.

The light brown yet darker daughter
sits on the father's back porch
and reads a poem to the brown
yet whiter one under his arms.

There is no history in their eyes
only the ancestral trick light
pulling the cart out of the mud and war
with mules, peasants, and slaves.

There are ten thousand words
a father's fortune in their eyes:
hollow star, broken wheel, caboose,
wild horse, wings over blue pond.

---

[20] Charles Fort, from *We Did Not Fear The Father: New and Selected Poems*

Their father's pen replaces the hollow star
with a broken wheel and drops a whistle
on the train as wild horses graze
and stare at the wings above the blue pond.

There is no history in their eyes
only two daughters in the backyard
hidden under the cellar door.
This is their evening of metaphor.

XVIII

"Leave, the Lord Said,"

May 2013

Spring Conference

O Pioneers!, the featured book for this conference, evokes that novel's "fortunate country" and its pioneering spirit.

Yesterday, in his keynote, Dan O'Brien suggested we add to our list of pioneer heroes the name of Aldo Leopold, father of ecology. Our scripture for this morning also speaks today of pioneering, of venturing beyond the known world, and no one elucidates what that is like better than Cather.

She apparently learned from her scripture what many of the more vocal evangelists of today did not learn, that the gospel does not favor stay-at-home, family-first values; it favors the one who can leave security behind and forge ahead to new places, new relationships, new ideas. It favors the pioneer. All of her major characters must leave something behind.

In so much (all?) of her fiction, Willa Cather portrays the pioneer. In many novels and stories, the setting for that celebration of the pioneer is the great fact of the west: out where you could see the vision and courage and drive and tenacity of the pioneers who ventured westward.

There too, however, even in that same place, you could see the considerable lack of those very qualities in those who followed, and sometimes even accompanied the pioneers.

Here, then, is a peculiar fact: For any given pioneer, place may be all-important. (That, at least, is why Walter Prescott Webb began his study of the Great Plains with a lesson in geography in general and climate in particular.) But while place may be the theater for the pioneer drama, it is no guarantee of finding a pioneer spirit. Alexandra Bergson, this year's hero, may well embody the qualities of the pioneer, but not everyone who surrounds her in the same place does.

Out there somewhere—in the new world, in the wilds of Quebec or New Mexico, in Nebraska or Colorado, Blackhawk or Moonstone—there is always a road "wild and beautiful" (50), beckoning the pioneer spirit. But once that road is followed and that place settled, there are always the narrow and stultifying "social classifications" that "every child understood . . . perfectly."

The reverse side of "the road is all" would appear to be "discovery is doom!"

It is not a new observation now, 75 years after Henry Nash Smith, that the joys of undiscovered land are doomed to disappear the moment they are discovered, but it was an idea new in Cather's time, and so as much Cather's intellectual property as Frederick Jackson Turner's.

We have to conclude, then, that pioneering may have little to do with place, indeed may have nothing to do with it at all. Though often pursued geographically, by moving from place to place, pioneering is essentially a spiritual state, a state of being, a set of personal qualities, qualities such as the "power of application ...[the] rugged will" (28) extolled in Thea by Herr Wunsch in *Song of the Lark*. Such qualities may be found in the Dan O'Brien's of today as well as in the Annie Pavelka's of yesteryear, may loom ahead of us on the road or may, as in Thea's effect on Wunsch, be found in "a society long forgot" (28).

It is perhaps Cather's excellence as a portrayer of places, possibly the best America has so far offered, that has misled us into thinking she was much interested in place. Perhaps we should have known better. Didn't she write in *My Ántonia*, that the place was "Nothing but land; not a country at all but the materials out of which countries are made"? It was the making that captured her imagination.

There was, to be sure, an almost ironic fascination to be found in the fact that Cather almost always seemed to long to be wherever she wasn't. But I think the truth of her art is that she was far more interested in ideas, what she often called impressions, than in places. It was, in our case, the idea of the pioneer that fascinated her.

What a combination: a keen observer of place who didn't give a hang about it in itself, a philosopher who didn't seem to care a fig about ideas except as they came into being. In the embodiment of an idea, there was the drama of the characters lives and the power of Cather's impressions. And where an ideal came to be embodied in a character, there was a character capable of knowing and honoring a place.

I've been citing *The Song of the Lark* for three reasons. The two incidental reasons are, one, because I happen to be re-reading it just now in preparation for the seminar in Arizona and, two, because I think we too seldom put side-by-side *O Pioneers!* and *Song of the Lark*. But the central reason is because of a remarkable passage that indicates something of how Cather found her truest portrait of the pioneer spirit.

Ray Kennedy has been talking to "Thee" (in Quaker terms, Ray's term for Thea would make of her an idealized audience), expounding his idea of how the cliff dwellers began to dwell in the cliffs. He has discounted them carving out dwellings because, in his view, they did not know how to work metals. "I guess civilization proper began when men mastered metals." Whatever learned opinions to the contrary were current at the time have given Ray "disrespect for learning" (106).

Not even a sentence intervenes before Cather turns this discussion on its head. I'll quote here nearly in full her next paragraph:

> Ray was not vain about his bookish phrases. He did not use them to show off, but because they seemed to him more adequate than colloquial speech. He felt strongly about these things, and groped for words, as he said, "to express himself." He had the lamentable American belief that

> "expression" is obligatory. He still carried in his trunk, among the unrelated possessions of a railroad man, a notebook on the title-page of which was written "Impressions on First Viewing the Grand Cañon, Ray H. Kennedy." The pages of that book were like a battlefield; the labouring author had fallen back from metaphor after metaphor, abandoned position after position. He would have admitted that the art of forging metals was nothing to this treacherous business of recording impressions, in which the material you were so full of vanished mysteriously under your striving hand. (107)

Ah! Now we have it: The writer as pioneer, our author as hero, the spirit of the pioneer even more necessary to the artist's journey across the page or canvas than journeys across the seas or the plains, the discovery of new words more epic than the discovery of places.

Again, we might have known. After all, there is hardly a place Cather evokes that had not been occupied before her characters arrived there, while to come upon one's impressions and the task of putting them into words is to enter virgin territory indeed. No old metaphors, no old positions, no old classifications will do. One must leave home! Which of her heroes did not?

We can't imagine that the scripture she knew had failed to inform her idea.

So, as we read this morning, (Genesis 12:1-4) the story of Abram—where the message to him is clear: first leave behind all you have known, then you might become a blessing.

So, Paul (Hebrews 12:1-3)—to paraphrase him: throw off the extra baggage and, by the way, keep your eye on the pioneer!

So Jesus (Matthew 5:21-26)—one of his constant messages: stop taking refuge in what you've heard all your life, what you are accustomed to and comfortable with. You will pay every last penny if you stay in that prison.

So our hymns— (#558) there is always danger, always woe—forward anyway.

Don't let the prospect of disaster stop you—be valiant (#563). Awake from your sleep, your ease, the lark is in the sky (#156).[21]

So in the fiction, as well:

> The wrestling with recalcitrant brothers and obdurate dirt and lonely longing of *O Pioneers!*
> The founding of convents and cathedrals and the epiphanies in strange caves and landscapes of the "catholic" novels.
> The slave girl on her way, away from Sapphira's world to a new voice, a new life. Ántonia's country girls who had to make their way as strangers in a strange land
> So the numerous evocations in her fiction of the birth of Jesus—about whom the old hymn extolled: "Thou shalt leave thy throne and the kingly crown."

And, so, Cather herself:

Her evident interest in the pioneering spirit of religious figures, especially here: Sister Hanna, Bishop Clarkson, Bishop Beecher, Fr. John Mallory Bates.

Her apparent fascination with the mural of the Ascension in the parish of that name in New York—always a leaving behind, always a venturing forth, many times more difficult in matters of faith and art than in matters merely of motion.

So, too, her leaving behind rigid classifications of past and present, male and female, home and away.

Arriving home to see it for the first time (long before Eliot coined the phrase)

---

[21] These hymn numbers are from *The Hymnal 1940*.

Then, dismantling the house.
Getting rid of much of the furniture, the novel d'meuble, indeed!

Embracing new kindred, a new tribe.

Moving on even after the world breaks in two.

And after Cather:

Mildred Bennett and the first board, Bernice Slote and the first teachers, Virgil Albertini and Steve Shively and the first *Teaching Cather*, Pat Phillips and the first stars at spring conference, Betty Kort and the first renovation, Jay Yost and the first professional annual report, Tom Gallagher and the first walking tour of New York, Merrill Skaggs and the first Drew conference; Bruce Baker, Ann Romines, Bob Thacker, and John Murphy and the first international seminars, Joel Geyer and Ron Hull and the first public broadcasting recognition, David Porter and the first Ives piano performance, Sue Rosowski and Guy Reynolds and the first Cather Project, Jim Fitzgibbon and the first prairie restoration, Andrew Jewell and Janis Stout and the first letters, Melissa Homestead and Leslie Levy and the first one hundred years of *O Pioneers!*

Leave, the Lord said; then I can make you great and make your name respected. O fortunate country that knows such pioneers!

THE REV. JOHN M. BATES

XIX

Providence and Plentitude

June 7, 2014

Spring Conference

Tolstoy, by whom Cather was much influenced, asked, "How much land must a man own?" The answer may in some measure depend not so much on the person, or his or her perceived needs, or even the social ecology of the community and the role land might play in it, but more on the geological and botanical and zoological character of the land, the character which so fills Cather's writing.

There we find the Nebraska prairie, the Arizona desert mesas, the Quebec rock and forest, Virginia's rolling hills—and in all of these richly described locations we find that the constant is the tragic-comic nature of humankind, being both possessor of the land and by the land possessed. "We were the land's before the land was ours," wrote Robert Frost, one of the poets she most admired.

It is not hard to see Cather as our Tolstoy (with Faulkner our Dostoyevsky and Hemingway our Turgenev), but I doubt those comparisons are original to me, nor are they, I imagine, entirely fair to other writers and the other parallels we could draw.

But it is fair to say, I think, that within or outside of literary traditions, nature has of late loomed up more largely in our range of attention than it did only a few short decades ago when most people could either ignore it or take it for granted. That is, we ignored or took it for granted until it became imperiled, and its peril has gradually started calling us to attention. If *Katie Couric Reports* has discovered the peril, we are imperiled indeed!

And the nature to which we now attend is neither the idyllic world of pastoral literature nor the world "red in tooth and claw" that followed the Darwinian awakening, but nature itself, as nearly as we can grasp it; that is, nature as we grasp it through an environmental understanding, through an ecological imagination.

I recently ran across one possible gauge of the place nature holds in our hearts today. Writing of his role as a bombardier on the first flight into Baghdad at the outset of the Iraq invasion, Jason Armagost catalogues for us the books he has taken along in his book bag, his reading for the long, cold flight. Among his list are these titles:

> David Petersen's *Heartsblood*, Jim Harrison's *Just Before Dark*, Ted Kooser's *Winter Morning Walks*, Billy Collins's *Nine Horses*, Wendell Berry's *A Timbered Choir*, Rick Bass's *Winter*, Edward Abbey's *A Voice Crying in the Wilderness*, Dean Toges's *Hunting the Osage Bow*, Saint-Exupery's *Wind, Sand, and Stars*, Thomas McGuane's *A Life in Fishing*

That's quite a lot of reading about nature, environment, and our relation to it and within it.

At the same time, it seems equally fair to say that both our appreciation for and understanding of religion continues to wane. Whether seen in declines in active participation in churches or in the plentiful discussions of atheism along the theme "the no's have it," it appears the average young bombardier would rather be solaced by recollections of his home in nature than exhortations of his home in heaven.

I would add that, with certain qualifications of course, I tend to agree with Armogast's reading list, certainly preferring it to the books I browsed on a recent visit to what calls itself a Christian bookstore.

It is similarly not easy to pigeonhole Cather. She seemed to take seriously her and her family's confirmation into the Episcopal Church here in Grace Church where we are gathered this morning, and she found much to admire in Ascension Church, New York, where she sometimes worshiped. She did not find enough there, however, to make her even sign up as a member, and one finds in her an undeniable grain of skepticism.

Addressing "Little Neddins" Gere about her stay with the Axtells when she first moved to Pittsburgh, she would write, "When I get through going to church and telling Indian stories I will have no more sense of truth left . . ." That letter was written July 27, 1896, and I don't see that sentiment or spirit abating across her lifetime. Cather seems to have sensed something like the saying on a coffee cup making the rounds: spirituality is a relationship to the holy, religion is crowd control.

However, despite her skepticism regarding organized religion and the doctrinal differences in which it specializes, Cather always exhibited a profound spiritual sense of an ultimate creative force and moral authority. She might demur from rigid and narrow definitions of that mystery (witness "Eric Hermannson's Soul") but she just as eagerly embraced the sort of spirituality that fosters reason, tolerance, and compassion (three elements Guy Reynolds noted regarding her appreciation of the faith of her Archbishop).

Throughout my reading of Cather over the past quarter century, it has struck me that most of her work could be seen as variation on endless combinations of land, pioneer, art, and faith. In our reading, we watch the land become, as Julene Bair noted, sometimes a character and always a shaper of character, see the artist who pioneers, catch the ways in which the land as well as prayer can be seen as sacred.

It is no surprise, then, that Cather's works find their way not only into standard places such as classes in American Literature, but also into courses in environmental literature, immigrant experience, feminist and LGBT writing, as well as into discussions of narrative, style, and genre as positions on an ideological spectrum.

This gathering does not need a lengthy discourse on Cather's relationship to these themes. Last year we followed her portrait of the pioneer, and this year we are following her artistic appreciation of the land, of natural forces, of the delicate balance of life. No doubt we have or will hear of her descriptions of the land, of how she sets an artistic and possibly sexual awakening in Walnut Canyon, a canyon of which she knew every inch and every shadow of change, or how the measure of the granite for the Archbishop's cathedral are the rock temples of the Navajo's desert. Our Cather Prairie is but a remnant of The Prairie she made famous. Her letters show her descriptions of the colors of wines, colors coming from the fields, the wine like wild flowers, and her joy in being in Paris but her greater joy of living by the Seine.

What is not so often discussed, however, is the perspective her religious connections and understanding might have given to her views of nature and the place in it for human endeavor and icons of holiness.

Our lessons this morning allow us, at least in a small way, to suggest a perspective that I believe would easily be further established in subsequent discussions of her texts.

I chose the lessons directly from the *Book of Common Prayer* that Cather would have last known, that of 1928, and from the lessons that prayer book set aside for what it called Rogation, days set apart for the periodic observation of creation, stewardship of the land, the preservation of natural resources in the encounter with agricultural enterprises. In the religious calendar Cather knew, these Rogation days joined Thanksgiving as days for pointed reflection on the relationship of God and people, planting and harvest, soil and nurture.

The lesson from Luke (Luke 11:5-15 Common English Bible) establishes a biblical commonplace: God's providence can only be characterized as a "plentitude"—there is no scarcity in Eden, no limit to creation's abundance, no measure of the giver except as extraordinarily prodigal in the giving. Here comes to mind the Hudson line Clay Jenkinson cited: "an eternity of abundance." And more, as the oddly out of place last verse suggests, when the human spirit is rightly attuned to this divine plentitude, then even those that life has muted find their voice. Not surprising teaching from the Jesus who said, "If you be silent, even the stones will sing." There is something profound here about the well-being of the community, the inclusion of the marginalized, and a reverence for the natural world.

That very promising, very hopeful lesson does not stand alone. It is paired with Ezekiel (Ezekiel 34:25-30 New International Version), one of the four great prophetic voices of the Hebrew scripture, something of a prequel to Luke with an added variation to the theme. Ezekiel, too, envisions a peaceable kingdom of plenty, also formed by a covenant, an agreement between human and divine wills, but Ezekiel adds that the way to this abundance-producing relationship requires ridding the land of its devouring wild beasts, not such as buffalo, elk, wolves, or the so-called "savages" settlement removed, but in fact later identified by Ezekiel as famine and shame, clearly beasts for whose behavior we humans are responsible!

The Rogation message—its perspective on an environmental imagination—comes in the pairing: abundance is God's doing, scarcity is ours. Cut down the rain forest, then don't be surprised if you get drought. We human beings turn out to be the sometimes evil and often devouring beasts, perpetrating famine and scorn, with (as the old hymn had it) "the whole realm of nature ours," that is, sadly, as our prey.

Who knew that such a contemporary understanding would actually be an ancient understanding, and a biblical one at that? I'm proposing that Cather did. Why else does she hold her characters responsible? Why else are her landscapes integral to her characters? How else understand her letter to Dorothy Canfield Fisher (March 15, 1916), protesting about Thea Kronberg and *Song of the Lark* that "my point was not the development of a genius—my point is always Moonstone." Because, of course, Moonstone is not in *Song of the Lark* so much a village as the hub of Thea's explorations and acquaintance with her surroundings—the seasons, the land, the place. In other words, as in Julene Bair's title, it is about "love and reckoning."

If Cather did not get this from our scripture today, she could have gotten it almost anywhere else in the scripture as the reading of the lessons in her church would have presented it. She could begin with the circumscription of Eden by four rivers, the idyllic encompassed by the natural. She could have seen in the Eden story the preference for living closely with nature that made for suspicion of the agricultural life of the plains, with its canals in place of rivers and its granaries guarded by snakes. She could have found it in Jesus' preference for parables drawn from the world of planting and harvesting. In the scripture as a whole, "all things come of thee O Lord."

In the same vein, regardless of the odd interview Cather gave the *New York Times* cited yesterday by Clay Jenkinson, where her own work was concerned, Cather thanks Elizabeth Shipley Sergeant (April 22, 1923) for understanding that the heart of *O Pioneers!* is "the country itself." She writes, "It's a fluid black soil that runs through your fingers, composed not by the decay of big vegetation but of the light ashes of grass. It's all soft and somehow that influences the mood in which one writes of it." Or, as she writes in *O Pioneers!*, "The great fact was the land itself."

Cather knew her scripture much like she knew most things, not in a superficial mastery of trivial details but in a keen and intuitive grasp of what lies at the heart of it, how it resonates with life. If for her the scripture was not so much a proof text as a portal, it was portal to seeing how rich and fragile is the world around us…as rich and fragile as the world within us, both worlds created by and badly in need of Grace.

XX

"Something Longer Lasting"

June 6, 2015

Spring Conference

We are gathered in the place, as Richard Norton Smith phrased it yesterday evening, "that did so much to define [Cather's] character before it populated her novels." And we are gathered on a historic occasion, the 60th anniversary of the Cather Spring Conference and the activities Mildred Bennett engendered. So, I suspect you may be wondering what the strange collection of lessons that we heard this morning has to do with our gathering here today, what the lessons could possibly have to do with the Spring Conference portion of the 2015 Cather International Seminar: Fragments of Desire: Cather and the Arts.[22]

Yet, doesn't that theme, our theme, Fragments of Desire, raise issues of the fragmentary and fleeting vis the lasting and sustaining, of beauty that is passing and the sorts of beauty that are lasting, of our passing desires and our heart's true longing, of incidentals and, as

---

[22] The scripture for this homily and service: I Samuel 8:4-15, 16-20; 11:14-15; Psalm 138; 2 Corinthians 4:13-5:1; Mark 3:20-35. On this historic occasion, Bishop J. Scott Barker was the celebrant. In giving personal attention to Grace Church, Bishop Barker was following suit of some of his predecessors, especially Bishop Joe Burnett, who included Grace in the list of those ministries and institutions that have enjoyed the support of the Sower Fund of the Diocese of Nebraska. The full list of those assisting Bishop Barker: Fr. Chuck Peek, Preacher; Dr. Steve Shively, Chaplain; Dr. Daryl Palmer, Lector. These, also, follow the precedent set by clergy, including Fr. Brent Bohlke and then Deans of St. Mark's Pro-Cathedral in Hastings, and, among the laity, Barbara Sprague, who played for many services on the little pump organ, and John English, who led the St. Juliana Choir in their presence at these services for many years.

Guy Noir puts it, life's persistent questions? Or as Corinthians has it, there's outward life where all is in disarray or decay but there is also an inward life capable of endless renewal.

Questions such as these are at the heart of all religious life, and so at the heart of the perpetual dialog between religion and the world—and our lessons help display the differences between the "passing show," the shadow world of Plato's cave, and eternity and its ways of breaking through into our lives, our world.

So I suppose if this sermon had a text it would be "what can be seen is temporary, what cannot is eternal" (II Corinthians 4:18)

On the one hand there is the transitory.

That might be political machination—as in the clamor for a King, especially as it is presented in I Samuel as motivated by the desire to be like other nations and a fear of standing up and doing the things we ought to for ourselves. We should note that, despite Samuel's catalogue of the ills that will ensue, the crowd gets its way, Israel gets a king and many more to follow. I am no Old Testament historian, but by my count there may have in that long history of kings been one and one-half decent leaders—which may explain why at the end of our lesson only the first King, Saul, is laughing knowingly, along with the blind crowd laughing because it has not yet learned any better. And hearing this lesson this morning, we might be forgiven for wondering if very much has actually changed!

Or, if we have completely shut off political life, we still might find the transitory in Paul's notice of our natural decay and affliction—which of us does not feel more of that as we grow older, which of us did not begin to get a sense for that even as children?

Many in Nebraska's book community have had reason lately to mourn the transitoriness of life, the natural decay we all face, occasioned for us this time by the untimely death of Dr. Mike Cartwright (long time member of the Sandoz Society, organizer of several of our Nebraska Book Festivals, reader of books for the blind, and fine teacher and scholar). On the day I received news of

Mike's death, I chanced on this poem, a poem that captures the "dust to dust" nature of our lives:

"Humans Regenerate All New Skin Every Seven Years" by Devin Murphy.

I'm 35, and have slipped my skin five times
Each I imagine breaking at the back of the
neck like a pit viper's – crawling and
pitching forward, though I know it all happened
flake by flake, first losing the touch
of my father, his hand resting on my chest to calm
me wailing and red in a crib, then my grip upon the
stick I swung and dislodged my little brother's right
eye, at some point the hard warm feel of my first lover's
inner thigh upon my lips drifted away, and that barb of
spiny coral fish piercing my sole and inflaming the muscles
until I was feverish from four days in the tropics, and now
my fingertips upon the wild and holy pulse of my son in the
night, where will that go, as it is this touch, finally this touch
that makes me long for my old skins to pick themselves off
the floor and wrap me so I can feel it all again, this time slower
this time knowing the body's slow, disrobing waltz.

Yes, the "slow, disrobing waltz" captures it all quite well, doesn't it!

Or, yet again, we may experience the transitory, the drive toward fragmentation and division, as it is found in Jesus' calling attention to families and kingdoms divided within themselves, surely not irrelevant to many concerns for the American family and to the horrible difficulties in reconciling beleaguered police and beleaguered minorities in our own divided kingdom.

Surely, in any "real politic," this is the real, the actual, the state of things, and it is sometimes so prevalent in our perspective that we wonder if that is all there is.

Yet our lessons also point to another reality, one that, despite most of our experience in this world, we can't shake—the ephemeral reality of something longer lasting, more permanent, more true.

Our Psalm tell us that is what we enshrine in the songs we love, what we find in loving and faithful relationships, the sort that sustain us, give us strength and hope, and our feeling in their grip that they are somehow stronger than kings, more powerful than troubles.

That is Paul's vision in II Corinthians: a weight of glory that outweighs any pain or strife, a conviction resting in what cannot be seen. Elsewhere, Paul writes (I Cor. 2:9): "Eye hath not seen, nor ear heard, neither have entered into the heart of man, the things which God hath prepared for them that love Him."

Faith communities locate that other reality in eternity, in God, in divine ideals. But even so—even as something seeming to be impossible outside our world, other than our experience—it has a way of breaking through into our lives, our world.

That is, of course, what we love best about the Christmas story— the incarnation, the divine becoming human, the invasion of our planet, the coming of the stupendous stranger.

It is also the whole conception behind the sacraments in general and the sacrament we celebrate today, the Eucharist, which an old hymn heralded as "o what a foretaste of heaven divine."

But the ways in which something eternal breaks into our world are not the confined to religions or churches. Foretastes of heaven divine fall on the just and the unjust, the sacred and the secular, the church and the world. And one of the most noted of these venues, these vehicles, is art. As A. P. Andrews noted in yesterday's panel, those charged with the care of our souls are sometimes preachers, sometimes artists.

It is no wonder there developed a religion of art. Cather pays such art homage in the passage from *Song of the Lark* when Thea asks, "What was any art but an effort to make a sheath, a mould in which to imprison for a moment the shining, elusive element which is life itself—life hurrying past us and running away, too strong to stop, too sweet to lose?" (279, close of part III of The Ancient People).[23]

23

It is in that vein that Cather, writing in *The Professor's House*, could portray Godfrey St. Peter replying to a student's comment at the end of one of his lectures: "Science hasn't given us any new amazements . . . any richer pleasures . . . not one! Indeed, it takes our old ones away . . . I don't think you help people by making their conduct of no importance—you impoverish them . . . Art and religion (they are the same thing, in the end, of course) have given man the only happiness he has ever had" (137-38, Library of the America's *Cather: Later Novels*).

And then there is that very interesting discussion in *Death Comes for the Archbishop*, when Bishop Jean Latour moderates Fr. Joseph Vaillant's preference for miracles by reminding him that "Where there is great love there are always miracles: (50). But, note, that comes at the conclusion of a chapter that tells us about the bell that the Archbishop hears ringing the Angelus (the same Angelus that John Murphy believes gives shape to the whole novel). Described as a "remarkable bell," there seems to be "no church tower in the place strong enough to hold it." It is the "good deal of silver in the bell" that "would account for its tone," and, as the Archbishop reminds Father Vaillant again, "the silver of the Spanish was really Moorish, was it not?" "The Spanish," Bishop Latour notes, "knew nothing about working silver except as they learned it from the Moors." The point is made pointedly enough that Fr. Vaillant replies, "What are you doing, Jean? Trying to make my bell out an infidel?" In his smiling reply, Latour presses on with the claim that "the introduction of the bell in the service . . . is really an adaptation of a Moslem custom." While Fr. Vaillant finds that "belittling," Latour insists it is just "the reverse" (43-45).

It is certainly not belittling to think that religion needs the vivid images of artistic creation and that art requires the considerable encounter with the depth of our being that lies at the heart of religious thought.

This homily was delivered during the 100th Anniversary of the publication of *The Song of the Lark*, and most Cather events in 2015 were noting or celebrating that novel.

So where does art, whether of bell-forging or ringing, end and religion, whether Moslem or the Angelus, begin? Were not both involved in the sound the Bishop hears and the meaning it imparts to him? The equation of art and religion, not so unusual in Cather's day, has fallen on harder times. Segments of the cultural and artistic communities are less easy with religion these days, and segments of the religious community are suspicious of art and culture. Cather's work is a good reminder that if what we are after is knowing the difference between the changes and chances of this mortal life and whatever glimpses of goodness and beauty transcend them, then both art and religion may serve "divine" purpose. Both reveal something of eternity breaking through into our lives in this world, offer us visions beyond the strifes and injuries of our world, give us at least fragments of our heart's deepest and truest desires. Indeed, as the old prayer put it, we find in religion and in art that which is greater than we either desire or deserve. On the plaque commemorating Cather at the Cathedral of St. John the Divine, the inscription reads: Thy will be done in art as it is in heaven. The kingdom not made with hands may well be found through art, through religion, or perhaps most through the miracle of what art and religion together reveal.

It was Paul Tillich, in his *The New Being* (a book that probably influenced a generation of preachers), who wrote, "We want only to communicate . . . an experience we have had that here and there in the world and now and then in ourselves [there] is a New Creation, usually hidden but sometimes manifest . . ." (18).

Interior of Grace Church showing the window memorializing the Rev. John Mallory Bates behind the altar.

XXI

"Paradise Revisited"

June 6, 2020

Digital Spring Conference During Covid

2020 Grace Church Homily, offered May 12 for airing June 6 as part of the digital Cather Spring Conference

Hello to all and thank you so much to Mother Mary Hendricks, conducting our service this morning, Dr. Steve Shively, reading our lessons and taking us later on a short tour of Grace Church, Tracy Tucker, offering us a look at some of the material in the National Willa Cather Center archives that tell us something of the life of Grace Church and bringing you good wishes from the Center, Carla Post for our music this morning from Grace Church's pump organ, and Nancy Peek who is behind the scenes helping Tracy with the filming and lighting.

If we think of the conference theme and keynote speaker, it is interesting that they parallel the themes for this time in the church calendar. We might well recognize that they are also the continuing themes in Great Plains Studies, themes we often explore here at this conference, themes drawn out by artists and scholars as they continue to confront the dynamic of the prairie: the lure of amber waves of grain, the fearfulness of the Great American Desert.

Among those themes, we readily note:

- the artist on the cusp of a new phase in her life
- the place of music and art in a full life
- the conflict in values between art and commerce
- both the pleasures and the harshness, the stewardship of or degradation of our physical surroundings
- and how the conditions in which we live affect our imaginations and sensibilities.

Lo and behold, these are all themes in Cather's *Youth and the Bright Medusa*!

All that history, all that critical commentary, all that studious writing and reading, replete in seven short stories! Think "Wagner Matinee," think "Sculptor's Funeral," think "Paul's Case," think—well, think of them all!

More and more, when I think of Cather, I'm reminded of assessments such as President Kennedy made when he told the Nobel prize winners assembled at the white house that they were the greatest assemblage of intellect to sit in the White House—since Jefferson sat there alone. Or of Alfred North Whitehead's definition of philosophy as a series of footnotes on Plato.

Think of the great work of contextualizing Cather—John Murphy's discourses on her acquaintance with art and religion, Guy Reynolds's on philosophy and anthropology, Ann Romines on gender and culture, Janis Stout and Andy Jewell's work to familiarize us with Cather's letters, Melissa Homestead's broadening our view of her friends and partners, and the wonderfully fresh look on her "becoming" in Daryl Palmer's newly published *Becoming Willa Cather*—not to mention the continuing work of the *Cather Review* and its contributors and editors (Tom Gallagher, Ann Romines, Bob Thacker, and Steve Shively).

Then think how all of that scholarship is simply the unpacking of the artistic and intellectual tour de force that is to be found in Cather's body of work.

No wonder Ferris Jabr ["The Story of Storytelling, *Harpers*, March 2019] calls stories "the most powerful and versatile skill in the human cognitive repertoire" (40). Jabr writes, "The world confronts the mind with myriad impressions, a profusion of other often perplexing beings, and an infinity of possible futures. The increasingly large brains of our ancestors, all the more attuned to the world's complexity, needed a way to organize this overwhelming torrent of information, to pass the multiplicity of experience through a reverse prism and distill it into a single coherent sequence. Stories were the solution" (40).

For now, let us overlook how Jabr's perception of "a profusion of other often perplexing beings" indicates that Jabr was either married with children and sheltering at home . . . or had attended gatherings of scholars and critics!

Let us note instead how Jabr's studies on the central importance of stories to our making sense of our lives and our world push us to see any great story-teller as part of a legacy of at least 100,000 years of story-telling in figures and symbols, to see the creative genius of anyone who makes new the few songs of the lark.

Not all stories, of course, get retold again and again, but the notes sung in them are sung again and again. Once, in a class on the Continental Novel, Professor Lee Lemon asked us to think of how few authors are ever known by very many readers or listeners for more than one or two pieces of work. His point was that to be remembered at all, even if for just one work, puts one in the pantheon of the gods of storytelling. Readers contemporary to the writer, of course, may rattle off several of their favorites, but time winnows down what lasts in the collective memory of the race. There must have been thousands of stories that died after their first telling—but we remember Little Red Riding Hood.

Betty Becker-Theye, translator, interpreter, and once the highest-ranking female academic official in Nebraska, argued that in all of literature there are only a handful of original characters. If you take your shoes off so you can count with both your fingers and toes, you can easily encompass the fresh representations of those characters. Among them you will find, in almost every category of hero or villain, thinker or doer, martyr or buffoon—the fresh creations of Willa Cather.

Take just one instance, the one I'm probably most fond of (with hopes that riding again this hobby horse will not quite exhaust some of your patience):

Let me suggest how much Cather belongs with those ancient storytellers who gave us the Garden of Eden story, one of the Ur stories of Western Civilization; how so much of Cather's work are her entry into the volume of case studies in Everyone's Paradise Lost.

First, of course, think briefly—mere mention is no doubt enough for Cather's reading audience—about how often and how much Cather made of biblical material, especially the creation story and, from later in Genesis, other foundational stories in what many scholars believe was a now lost Hebrew epic. I might note some of the many instances, some of which you are already thinking of:

- The sections of *My Ántonia* mirror the five books of the Hebrew scripture called the Pentateuch
- On the walk that entices Jim early on to venture out of the Burden farmyard, he echoes Jacob's awareness *(in both the ladder from heaven (chapter 28) and the wrestling with a divine manifestation (chapter 32)* of being where "the world ended"
- Jim Burden sitting down "in the middle of the garden, where snakes could scarcely approach unseen"
- Ántonia's supposed sin issues in her inheritance of both curses described as the consequence of losing Paradise: both labor in the field and labor in childbirth

Doesn't this, too, belong in our list: when Europeans 'discovered' what they liked to believe was a "new" world, they conceived of it as the new Eden, its principal occupant the New Adam, pointedly from their skewed reading of Genesis, not the new Eve, a feature captured in *My Ántonia* in the section title "Cuzak's Boys," a title we know is at odds with them being not Cuzak's but his wife's children, the first of them not his at all.

And this: Adam and Eve, in Hebrew mean simply Man and Woman—etymologically very much Man and Other Man. They walk in the garden conversing at cocktail hour with their host until they eat the fruit of the forbidden tree, and then they know they are naked and put on clothes, their brief moment in paradise gone. As we hear the story, it is hard not to hear echoing in our mind, from Virgil a world away, Optima dies prima fugit! At any rate, Cather heard the echo a century ago.

It is remarkable how often the parallels continue!
- The garden into which Jim and Ántonia wander in *My Ántonia* shifts to the Edenic copse, the orchard at the Forrester's in *A Lost Lady*. There the children witness the wanton cruelty of Poison Ivy which in turn provokes the beginning of Neil's disillusionment with what he thought was paradise
- The snake in the Garden is not far behind us when we get to *Death Comes for the Archbishop* and meet the villainous— Buck Scales!
- More subtly, there, too, we meet the suffering virtue of Old Sada. In the Hebrew, Sada means pure, chaste, fortunate, blessed, and princess, and is a name cognate with Sarai and Sarah, meaning "mother to us all," which takes us back to Genesis's chronicle of matriarchs and patriarchs beginning with Abraham and Sarah. Does it tell us something about Ur stories that Sada carries the same meaning and the same cognates as it does in the languages of the Middle East as it does in both the Japanese and Yoruban languages.
- And perhaps we might also note that "Paul's Case" also appeared in a garden, *The Troll Garden* of Kingsley, Rossetti, and Cather's re-collection.

In sum: if the Garden of Eden story were not still, then and now, informing our thinking both as a conception of self and of society, then *The Scarlet Letter* would have been impossible and the imagery in Cather's fiction unfathomable, even perhaps her choice of the name Eden in *Youth and the Bright Medusa*.

When we identify with her stories, it is because they are as ancient as the story of civilization itself, just as the Book of Genesis preserves its fundamental and universal story. The world's great legends and lore, myths and tales, were not unknown to Cather, an astute student of the human condition.

No pestilence is any respecter of persons, but then no story is dependent on the conditions under which it continues to be told. Cather's stories survive!

Ezra Pound had told the new women and new men of an emerging century to make it new. And so Cather did. By the grace of God and the work of both the Foundation here and its sister Cather project in Lincoln, and from the cusp of 1920 and *Youth and the Bright Medusa*, to the cusp of 2020, Cather's reputation continues to grow, her place on the Olympus of Stories seems secure, and her work continues to challenge us to deeper understanding of history and culture, body and soul, normal and extraordinary!

Amen.

XXII

"Lost and Found"

June 3, 2023*

Spring Conference

Probably, knowing we'd be spending time with A Lost Lady, we've all been thinking a bit about the lost and found departments in life, the life of Cather's characters and our own lives.

To lose sight of something, for a moment at least and sometimes for a lifetime, is to lose that something. We connect sight and finding, loss of sight and losing, our relationship to what is lost or found so naturally that we don't even notice the connection, but that connection underlies many of the parables of Jesus and those actions of Jesus that the Gospels treat as parables.

Lostness and Foundness. Those words for a condition are usually rendered as The Lost and the Found, as in the phrase from Jesus best-known parable and the popular hymn derived from it, "was lost but now am found/was blind and now I see."

Let's think together of Cather's story.

You will recall that, at one point, the narrator, watching Niel follow Daniel Forrester's slow progress on two canes, remarks, "He looked like an old tree walking" (115). It was, if I recall 30 years ago when I first preached on this, and at that time I noted that this would be a strange simile if it were not a direct allusion to an equally strange parallel from the Gospel of Mark, where the context enlightens us as to Cather's use of the allusion.

They came to Bethsaida. And some people brought to him a blind man, and begged him to touch him. And he took the blind man by the hand, and led him out of the village; and when he had spit on his eyes and laid his hands upon him, he asked him, 'Do you see anything?' And he looked up and said, 'I see men; but they look like trees, walking.' Then again he lad his hands upon his eyes; and he looked intently and was restored, and saw everything clearly. And he sent him away to his home, saying, 'Do not even enter the village' (Mark 8:22-26 RSV).

The allusion, of course, is to the moment between the two phases of the man's sight being restored, the moment when he sees men but they look like walking trees, but the allusion is only a means to an end, the means of drawing the full healing story to bear on A Lost Lady, for the outline of the biblical story is woven into Cather's account of Niel and Mrs. Forrester, the irony in Cather's exposure of who really is lost and who found, who sees and who does not.

Twice, each time positioning Niel as a voyeur to a scene, thus keeping the motif of sight in front of the reader, Niel encounters Mrs. Forrester in the embrace of some man not her husband, once Frank Ellinger, then Poison Ivy. Each encounter is what, keeping with the theme, I think we'd call an "eye-opener" for Niel, who begins to marvel at how well the Captain knows his wife. Between the two eye-openers, Cather places the remark about Captain Forrester appearing like a tree walking. That is, Cather places the remark in the novel just where it is placed in the biblical story, between two phases of a process of eye opening.

After the first encounter, Niel throws the flowers he has picked into the mud, and after the second he retraces his steps by that mud where he had thrown the flowers the first time. Cather must have noticed that in Matthew's gospel, Mark's spit becomes Matthew's mud. As if the introduction of the spit/mud motif would possibly still not be enough, Cather gives us a glimpse into what Niel is thinking, "It took two doses to cure him. Well, he had had them" (170).

Now all literary allusions have their limits. Here, Cather inscribes the scriptural text into her own, not for many of the biblical themes but only for one…not for instance for any theme of 'holiness' or moral ideals, but only for the applicability of the themes of blindness and sightedness to a story abounding in ironies about who or what is lost.

The allusion is one of the many ways we readers are alerted to how *A Lost Lady* is a novel of many blindnesses, of losing sight of something precious. There is Neil's blindness to seeing any individuality in the other boys, to seeing anything genuine in the townswomen's concern for Marion, to seeing Marion age; blindness to the fact of her fears or to accepting them as part of her, to seeing how the past might apply to the present, or to seeing the sexuality of Marion Forrester; blindness especially to grasping with any comprehension her "power to live" (125, 171).

But Niel's are not the only instances of blindness. There is also the blindness of the upper classes to the plight of the lower, the blindness of the lower classes to the artificiality of the barriers which exclude them (as for instance when Adolph 'wouldn't come to the funeral' (145). And what of the blindness of the other stock-holders to their duty when the financial institution fails? What of the blindness of supposed old friends to Mrs. Forrester's subsequent needs? How many lose sight of how much?

Of course, we often don't see what we aren't looking for. Many of you will know the story of thousands of passengers passing by the dozens of street musicians that play at the stations of the subway in New York, none noticing at first that one of the players was none other than Joshua Bell. Sometimes we don't see what is in plain sight…just one of the many dimensions of sightedness and blindness.

At the time I first preached on this, I was reminded of a wonderful Annie Dillard essay on 'sight and insight,' where she discusses the case of people who have been blind and, then, through surgery, begin to recover their sight—about how they come to see and how they value seeing.

I recalled then how a student of mine, working with that essay, was struck by Dillard's description how such people at first see objects and their shadows as "color-patches" and "dark marks." He wrote in his response statement to his reading, "Those people have taught me to see the world as a dazzle . . . We need to express what we see . . . blurt out the . . . words, oh God! How beautiful! We need to speak well of the world." Surely, a very similar response follows a close reading of A Lost Lady.

This year, approaching A Lost Lady yet again, I've been delving into Nicholas Humphrey's theory of the mind in his new book, Sentience. There, studying how two separate portions of the brain govern our seeing, explaining why we can sense even without seeing, and see even without sensing.

For instance, we see a loved one walk into the room (perception) and we feel something about that entrance (sensation). But notice this: we can feel the same thing day-dreaming about a loved one walking into the room, seeing it only with our mind's eye. Or, famously, people still feel pain in a leg that has been amputated.

Humphrey coined a word for this: he calls it blindsight, and here's his point: blindsight, in his view, is the seat of our ability to empathize with other's joys and pains…in other words, empathy consists in using our own experience to acknowledge the humanity in others. Our sensations, our sentience, is at the root of how we evolved from brutishness to caring.

Surprise! Without the benefit of Humphrey's studies, this is precisely how Cather treats the contrast between losing sight of and getting insight into others…it is what shapes A Lost Lady, in the same way in which discourses on what it means to be a neighbor inform Obscure Destinies.

Cather starts with what seems given, the blindness, especially that of others, as seen by Niel. But, in a formula she perfected in My Ántonia, we then learn something of Niel's own blindness. And that, in a kind of double effect, leads us to question his reliability, to question the credibility of his view of the blindness of others.

We, the readers, also receive "two doses," one healing in two phases. A Lost Lady and the scripture inscribed in it call us to cultivate the disposition to take second looks, not to be satisfied with what things look like, to pierce through appearances to see, to find what things really are, to find the lost, or perhaps to find it—or they—were never lost at all except to our own blindness, to having been blind, now to see, and to find ourselves in finding the lost.

Amen.

* I had approached A Lost Lady in a Grace Church sermon given in 1991. A passage from that sermon was not relevant to this, but might serve as a further comment:

In a parallel passage in Matthew's Gospel, instead of spit, Jesus is said to use mud. The use of spit or mud becomes almost a trope, such that one often hears homilies that conflate the two stories, confusing the two.

Indeed, A Lost Lady is a veritable catalog of ways to be blind, all emblemized in the little bird Ivy Peters blinds. We see the malice of the act before we understand how it provides emphasis to the portraits of the willing blindness of the human participants to the novel's action. How often, as in Niel's averted gaze, they seem to fear clear sight. Like Sgt. Schultz of the old sitcom Hogan's Heroes, they "see nothing." But here, the Schultz's are not very loveable and the situation is far from comic.

The novel couples blindness and fear in the tension known in small towns and small neighborhoods, the tension between knowing (even nosing around) so much, and yet fearing what we will see, who will see us, what the neighbors will think, how seeing will lead to judging.

All this blindness is played off in the novel with the comments about and instances of Captain Forrester's clear-sightedness. As the structural counterpoint shows the dangers of blindness and commends the benefits of sight, the rhetoric of the novel serves to draw the reader into scorning blindness and coming to a new appreciation of sight.

The novel may tell a very personal and domestic story, but that story is a call to look again at the perennial problem of caste and class, the plague that stalked at the high-noon of the frontier west, and still plagues us in the noonday of our own times.

And there is still a bit more. In Mark the strange healing falls between two misunderstandings, two blindnesses if you will: the disciples' failure to understand the meaning of the feeding of the 5000 on the one hand and their similar failure to understand the nature or necessity of Jesus' own suffering. Similarly, in Cather's novel Niel's eye-opening encounters fall between Mrs. Forrester feeding the boys in the grove on the one hand and her own suffering on the other.

Niel misunderstands both of these scenes in some significant way. This of course makes Mrs. Forrester the "Christ figure" of the novel and Niel the "blind" disciple, which, if it did nothing else, would heighten our sense of losing and finding.

XXIII

"A Dwelling in which God Lives"

June 7, 2025*

Cather Spring Conference

The Venerable Bede, the first writer to identify himself as being English, scolded the church for its sin of luxuriating in good times and so being ill-prepared for what may come. What was then to come was the Viking invasion! Or in later history, when what came was human chattel slavery and the weakness of colonial Christianity, divided by denominations, to resist or combat it.

In contrast, Bede extols those saints who exemplified justice, devotion, peace, and charity. In the middle of this exhortation, in historian Peter Ackroyd's words, Bede points to "the remnants of churches . . . where the ruins still stood . . . [whose] walls are to be seen still standing and . . . every year miraculous cures are wrought" in such a place.

Miraculous cures in such a place! Well, here we are today within a set of still standing walls, so I'd venture to say we might possibly be in for a surprising day!

It would be 900 years after Bede before John Webster, in *The Duchess of Malfi*, would have Antonio declare "I do love these ancient ruines;/We do never tread upon them, but we set/Our foot upon some reverend history."

Later, William of Malmesbury carried Bede's narrative further, lamenting, "how great was the disgrace, how grievous the sickness brought upon England, by the eclipse of education and the depravity of wicked men." Ackroyd asks us to consider if that is not the, "Same note sounding through the centuries"—centuries that would include our own! (All Ackroyd references are to Peter Ackroyd, *The English Soul: Faith of a Nation*)

Cather's built and natural environments, the theme of this spring's conference, bring us this morning to these walls, wherein we set our feet upon some reverend history, the reverend figure in our case being Willa Cather, another champion of justice and devotion and peace and charity, another voice whose work exhorted readers about the sometimes triumph of ignorance and greed, meanness and bigotry. What names she gave them: Buck Scales, Wick Cutter, Poison Ivy! Perhaps today we might think of other names.

As much as anywhere else in Red Cloud, or possibly anywhere else at all, this church, the sacred space within these walls, this built environment, ratified and enlightened and sustained the long song she sang in the stories and novels and poems that made her the very artist she'd envisioned at the age of 10, the age at which, in her letter to Roscoe she told him, "I knew that a great artist, a new kind of artist, would come out of 'the old peoples in a new world'." (June 5, 1914, p. 191 Letters)
The artist turned out to be Cather herself.

And, standing out against whatever evils are sufficient to the day, Cather portrays characters of sometimes continuous, sometimes more fleeting virtue, but real nonetheless. Often those of "obscure destinies," their spirit stood for something in the moral compass of the world and so often did so in a specific built or natural environment. Among the ways we recall Marian Forrester: her arriving in front of this very church in which we sit today.

Cather was following many old literary devices where a character symbolizes something larger. In Chaucer's "Nun's Priest's Tale" a widow, because of her virtues, stands also for the Church, her virtues extolled in actual churches, in the iconography of stained glass or no doubt less reliably in the preaching.

In the Nun's Priest telling of Chaucer's 'the road is all' tale:

> A widow poor, somewhat advanced in age,
> Lived, on a time, within a small cottage
> Beside a grove and standing down a dale.
> This widow . . . /Had led, with patience, her…simple life,
> . . .
> By husbanding of such as God had sent
> Of sharp sauce, why she needed no great deal,
> . . .
> For dainty morsel never passed her throat;
> . . .
> Repletion never made this woman sick;
> And no wine drank she,--either white or red;
> . . .
> A yard she had, enclosed all roundabout.

Like Cather, Chaucer, having noted that she was poor and old, starts his introduction of the widow with the built environment of her cottage and the natural environment of her grove, and then ends the prologue with her "yard . . . enclosed all roundabout."

The iconography of "widow" as "church" is, of course not a description of the Church at as it is always found, but rather of the Church as it ought to be, as it is called to be, as someone from time to time has to scourge it into being. In a dramatic action, Jesus enters a temple to throw out the money changers and declare that God's house is to be a house of prayer—for all people. His example would have to be repeated down through the ages, especially in times and places when humility is replaced by pomp, where integrity is hedged about by circumstances.

Chaucer's iconography is drawn from scriptural similes, the scriptures read this morning and the hymns drawn from them, where the writers of both were always seeking an analogy by which we could understand something of how God's presence could be found in an all-too-human institution—it's like a human body and its parts, it's like a family, like a garden, a field, a bride, a flock, and over and over again, like a temple, a house, a built environment.

In the Letter to the Church in Ephesus, the reference to God's household, its foundations being the Apostles and Prophets, its Cornerstone Christ himself, in [Whom], the whole building is joined together and rises to become a holy temple" and this followed by the assurance that "you too are being built together to become a dwelling in which God lives."

In their turn, these passages were echoing Jacob proclaiming a place "the house of God, the gate of heaven" (Genesis 28:16-17) or Moses portraying the Cloud of Glory as settling within walls of the temple (Exodus 29:42+), or Isaiah writing:

> "See, I lay a stone in Zion, a tested stone,
>   a precious cornerstone for a sure foundation;
> the one who relies on it
>   will never be stricken with panic" (28:16)

The Professor's House (being addressed here and soon again later this month in the symposium in Milwaukee), where only an outlander's vision brings the possibility of life into the story, a vision that proves to be short-lived even in Tom's own life, and seems not to find a lasting place in Godfrey St. Peter's built environment, his house, which is a site of lost dreams and misplaced values . . . its owner stricken with that form of panic Thoreau described as "quiet desperation," reminding me of the lament in *Obscure Destinies* over "the feeling of something broken that could so easily have been mended" (230).

In contrast, in Cather's *Not Under Forty*, she extols a "place where the past lived on—protected and cherished, had sanctuary from the noisy push of the present" (61). Saint Lily Tomlin put it this way when she joked that studies have shown reality to be our greatest cause of stress – for those of us who are in touch with it. Stress and panic or protection and sanctuary, always the choice of an Easter people living in a Good Friday world.

Or again, we hear Cather (119) proclaiming that what we "most love" is not "bizarre invention" but "the old story [being] brought home to us closer than ever before." 'Tell me the old, old story' up against one more Jardiance commercial! Keeping up a tradition rather than keeping up appearances.

Still, for all its tensions and oppositions, dreams fulfilled and dreams lost in every age, the present is always the place where we've been called to live—to live through if need be—where our courage and integrity are called for, shored up by the honest appraisals and clear thought that typify our love for arts and education, imagination and learning, especially as found in Cather's works, where the characters we admire, from aspiring singers to neighborly farmers, bear out the promise of life built on firm foundations, where it is so often the case that the stone the builders rejected is found to be the chief cornerstone.

Whether thinking of the mystical body or the built environment where God lives, what Cather seems to value is not so much doctrine or dogma and certainly not show or showiness. She valued places of transcendence, places where the story is kept alive, where beauty is seen as sacred, a place where the Cloud of Glory sometimes comes to rest among us, that holy house where we encounter people like us, flawed and faced with the fleetingness of life, but from time to time touched by eternity and made new, made whole, Cather noting that where there is great love there are always miracles.

Sometimes built environments join the natural world as places where, in John Muir's words, you can go to lose your mind and find your soul. Cather found built environments, here or in her imagination, where she could possess her soul, find purpose and solace, enter a dwelling in which God lives.

Here we are, just where Cather, her family, and close friends embraced humility and simplicity, the beauty of holiness, always present where God truly dwells, in a building or in a heart. And if a present and loving God and some reverend history prove to be enough, perhaps today, we leave here with the miracle of sufficient hope to meet an increasingly divided and hostile world. Just maybe, within these still standing walls and their own reverend history, we, too, are touched by Grace in Grace Church. Amen.

*This homily was a valedictory for me. Having begun organizing the Grace Church services, always at Spring Conference and sometimes for Cather's birthday celebrations, and now nearer 83 than 82 years of age, this was the year to pass back the responsibilities for this service to the Episcopal Diocese of Nebraska. My father, The Very Rev. George H. Peek, had preached here years ago and officiated at the burial of Cather's close friend Carrie Miner Sherwood when he was Dean of St. Mark's Pro-Cathedral in Hastings. (I would later preside over the Memorial for Helen Cather Southwick—see the Epilogue). Fr. Brent Bohlke, an Episcopal Priest and Cather scholar, conducted the services for years, and I took over when he left to be Chaplain at Bard. Many others have preached here over the years, including Frank Griswold, then Presiding Bishop of the Episcopal Church, and the Bishop of Nebraska, The Rt. Rev. J. Scott Barker. Over those years, this was one forum in which our church could realize its ecumenical vision; gatherings here have included non-believers, believers from other religions or denominations, Episcopalians, and the simply curious. The service was once Con-celebrated by me and Roman Catholic priest Charles Kelliher, who had been ordained in Red Cloud, his first Eucharistic celebration being at the altar now in St. Juliana's Church. Grace Church meant a lot to the Cather family; the service has meant a lot to locals, conference participants, including Cather scholars and conference invited speakers, and the Cather Foundation. It will continue through the leadership of Bishop Barker, Father Randy Goeke, Mother Mary Hendricks, Deacon Colleen Lewis, and Drs. Steve Shively, Daryl Palmer, and Nathan Tye and their successors. This part of my ministry has indeed been another way of participating in the Cather Foundation. It has been a blessing for well over 35 years, and I'm grateful to have been asked to make it part of my ministry and carry on in this way the work begun by Mildred Bennett in creating the Foundation and Bishops Clarkson and Beecher in establishing Grace Church. Thanks to the many Foundation figures who invited me in: Pat Phillips, Steve Ryan, Betty Kort, Leslie Levy, and currently Ashley Olson, Tracy Tucker, and Rachel Olsen.

Epilogue

"Generations"

August 14, 2004

Memorial Service for Helen Cather Southwick

In the name of the one God who creates us, redeems us, and sanctifies us. Amen.

About the time my mother must have been getting terribly uncomfortable during the last trimester of carrying me to birth, Helen Cather Southwick was getting married. As did my mother that summer, this same Helen Cather Southwick seems to have had a voracious appetite. At least Charlene Hoschouer recalls that Helen would be a fountain of conversation until the food arrived for a meal, whereupon she would suddenly become quiet, to concentrate on the business at hand. Apparently, she had a voracious appetite for more than food...but for family and heritage as well, for life itself. We come here today to celebrate the life of Helen Cather Southwick, who, toward the end of her life, said, "Tell my friends in Red Cloud I'll be there soon."

And so she is, here with us, all of us here to sit humbly with our God, in memory of her...we who are her family, or her friends, or her partners on the WCPM Board of Governors, of which she was, of course, an honorary member.[24]

This is one of those houses where we keep our appointments with God. Of course, God appears where and when he will, his presence quite likely felt keenly someplace one day and another place another

---

[24] Jim Southwick was to become a member and, additionally, to make many gifts to the Cather Archive, both in Red Cloud and at UNL.

day. But the scripture shows us that God seems to have a preference for his work to have some continuity, for his presence not to flit, however charismatically, but to abide, to endure among a people, in a place.

My salvation, we read in Isaiah 51:8, shall be from generation to generation, and in one of the Psalms (145:4) David proclaims, One generation shall praise thy works to another.

So important are these connections of one generation to another, this generational continuity, that for every patriarch beginning with Noah, the Bible concludes the story saying, and these were the generations (of Noah, of Jacob, of whoever), and Genesis (2:4) even figures for us the generations of the heavens.

There was a time when we connected more to the generations of our family, and a time when, because of that, we connected the generations of our family more to a place, even to a house…the old home, the homestead—the home that marked the family that marked the place.

That is less frequent now, for many reasons, but especially in the light of the changing times and manners, what a remarkable thing it is today, that a person baptized in this church in 1918 should come, 86 years later, to be memorialized in that same place. It is remarkable for Helen Cather Southwick, it is remarkable for Grace Church, and it is remarkable for us, gathered here today. And since it is so remarkable, we should remark on it.

The Cather family's connection to Red Cloud and Grace Church, Helen's connection to the family, her continuing connection through the Hoschouer's restoration of the second Cather home…these connections and continuities are signs of something significant.

Helen never forgot her family, for whom her love was unconditional, and they never forgot her. Letters went back and forth, extended visits took place. It was on one of Willa's extended visits that Helen was born and Willa was able to be present as one of her godmothers. And so it was, the family gathered and regathered, membered and remembered itself, down these many years. Helen certainly remembered Willa and Willa her.

In all that there is the striking impression that here were people who truly, as David proclaimed, praised God's works to each other from generation to generation. They shared the feeling for the pasture next to their home, for the horse that was kept there, for the lark, commemorated in Jules Breton's portrayal of the *Song of the Lark* that hung in the writer's studio once attached to the barn, and always the sweet smell of the hay that left its indelible impression on them all.

And as the generations remained constant to one another, so they became identified with and identified themselves with, the place, the home, the houses in which one another lived out the meaning of their several lives.

This was true of the house at Grand Manan, the only house Willa Cather ever owned outright, and which Helen restored.

It was true of the second Cather home here in Red Cloud, which Helen helped Charlene and Doug restore by virtually walking through all nineteen of its rooms in her memory, as well as from time to time passing on items she associated with her family, with those rooms, with her precious heritage.

And it is true of this house of worship to which one of its own former Sunday School students returns today to mark her entry into the life of perfect service, into that home not made with hands, into the land of light and joy where she may be led from strength to strength in life eternal. It is no stretch of the imagination to believe that even as we gather she is once again learning by heart the distinctive features of each of the mansions in her father's house, quite possibly adding a touch here and there as the Lord bids her be at home.

Willa Cather reminded Helen once in a letter that, on leaving the house here in red Cloud, Helen would gaily call out, "Goodbye, dear house."

From this house today, frequented generation to generation, where God's presence is still felt, still real, we gather to say, in song and prayer, "Goodbye, dear Helen."

Chuck Peek and Steve Shively at Washington National Cathedral

Appendix A

Remarks made, Friday, June 2, 2006, by Dr. Charles A. Peek, President of the Board of Governors of the Cather Foundation, on the occasion of the transfer of the Willa Cather Memorial Prairie from the Nature Conservancy to the Cather Foundation.

The gift of these 608 acres represents another phase in the partnership between the Nature Conservancy and the Cather Foundation, which share the goal of protecting the prairie and enhancing the educational opportunities it provides.

The photograph of the prairie that appears on the cover of the most recent edition of the *Willa Cather Newsletter & Review* also appeared on the cover of its 1974 edition. That newsletter was then celebrating the purchase of the Willa Cather Memorial Prairie by the Nature Conservancy, a purchase made possible by funding from the Woods Charitable Fund, Inc. of Lincoln, Nebraska, and Chicago, Illinois. Tom Woods of Lincoln, the Frank Woods of Chicago, and Lucia Woods of New York were present that day. Lucia, of course, took the photograph.

Lucia is very sorry she could not be here today. This prairie, a major source of Cather's writing, is dear to her, as it was to Mildred Bennett as well, whose "hand in this purchase," the *Newsletter* notes, "is obvious." Lucia sends her greetings to all of us here today and, on behalf of the Cather Foundation, I want to say to Lucia: without you and your family, none of this would be happening today. We miss you, and only wish you could have been here.

Under the leadership of Jim Fitzgibbon, Mark Illian, Joe Strickland, John Swift, Cheryl Swift, Joe Springer, Bill Beechley, Gilbert Adrian, Duane Linnerman, Dave Smith, and Ann Fisher-Worth, the Foundation will continue to preserve the prairie and the dream that Mildred, Lucia, and the Woods family shared.

Coming on two centuries ago, William Wordsworth wrote, "Getting and spending we lay waste our powers,/Little we see in nature that is ours."

When I was in school, we were taught that that last line merely meant that we had grown apart from nature, lost touch with its rhythms and beauties.

I have come to think Wordsworth was wiser than that and that the line means much more. We look around our material and social worlds and think, this can be ours. Just enough getting and spending, and we can wrest a world and happiness from it. But when we turn our eye to nature itself, we instinctively sense that it cannot be ours. Thus some become at best indifferent to and at worst hostile to nature.

Robert Frost captured this same idea when he told us we were the lands before the land was ours. And again, since we would rather own than be owned, would rather shape than be shaped, nature looms up for some as at best an intrusion and at worst an enemy.

There's plenty in the ecological record of the human race the last 200 years to suggest both Wordsworth and Frost were right, and their insights were Cather's as well. Early in *My Ántonia*, we see that both Jim and Grandmother get on rather well with nature precisely because, as my Chinese student Li Jing suggests, neither thinks nature exists solely to satisfy them.[25] And of course this particular system of nature we call prairie: did anyone ever capture it quite like Cather could? She knew this land when much more of it was wild grass prairie; watched as first some and then more of it was converted by the plow.

Of course, we humans have to eat, have to make a living, and only nature is there to serve that end. Gaining food and occupation are indeed often heroic tasks as Cather knew. But she seems to have known as well that, on this planet, two species depend on each other for their continuation as species, and those two are humans and grass. The domestication of cereal grasses has, to be sure, played the central role in the development of civilization; but we know, too,

---

[25] Li Jing's paper, an ecological view of Cather's novel, was referenced earlier in the Spring Conference in the panel on Teaching Cather Abroad.

that wild grass prairie, places of wilderness, deserve our conservancy, not as bits of nostalgia or as oddities, but as, if nothing else, holding secrets for human survival and harboring patterns and beauties vital for our souls.

I have no idea how Cather would feel about all our efforts to preserve her past. She herself abandoned her homes here for another life. I suspect she would have been pleased to see them preserved, the Opera House restored, and Grace Church maintained. But I am certain she would have been most pleased with the preservation of this prairie and with its transfer from the good stewards who have cared for it for over 30 years to the Cather Foundation. For many years, that work was the responsibility of Dr. Hal Nagel, who is present with us today.[26]

On behalf of the Foundation, I accept, then, this prairie, with great thanks to the Nature Conservancy for their work in general and this gift in particular, and with the promise that we will not only be good stewards of the prairie in our turn, but will model our stewardship on the good example set for all of us by Hal and the Nature Conservancy. We deeply appreciate the Nature Conservancy's gift to us and its trust in us. I suspect this prairie will, in now unsuspected ways, change our foundation for the better. After all, our foundation is trying to build something, too, and though this prairie is not a world, it is, as Cather taught us, the materials from which worlds are made.

---

[26] Hal Nagle and Helen Stauffer began a summer program for teachers and students, centered on Red Cloud, Cather, the Prairie, and the lore surrounding all of them; that ran its course and then was 'resurrected' by UNK with Chuck Peek, Mark Eifler, and Jim Fitzgibbon. We met in the unfortunately named "Man and the Land" building that housed Leonard Skov's ambitious project for continuing education in Red Cloud.

Cather Prairie

Appendix B

Grace Episcopal Church building, completed in 1883, owed much of its early activity to Sister Hannah, a faithful Episcopalian Deaconess and lay reader in charge of the development of an Episcopal presence in Red Cloud in the 1890s. Sister Hannah saw to the establishment of a guild, made sure there was a superintendent for the Sunday School, and raised the last $100 to pay the debt on the church lots. However, she could have little foreseen the future prominence given the church by the membership of its most illustrious parishioner, Willa Cather.

Among the founders of the church were Silas Garber, former governor of Nebraska, and his wife Lyra Wheeler Garber. Even their fame was to be enhanced by Cather's use of Lyra as the prototype for Marian Forrester, the main character of Cather's novel *A Lost Lady*.

The Cather family "migrated" to the Episcopal Church in 1906 when Willa's sister Elsie was baptized and confirmed. From then on the Cather marriages, confirmations, burials, baptism were Episcopalian. Willa served as godparent for her niece Helen's baptism in 1918; and, in December 1922, Willa Cather and her parents were formally confirmed by Bishop George Allen Beecher at Grace Church, shortly after the Bishop had served as master of ceremonies for the 50th wedding anniversary celebration of Willa's parents.

Her friendship with Bishop Beecher continued long after her last visit to Nebraska; the two communicated regularly by letters, and Bishop Beecher frequently dined with Cather when he was in New York. The last letters between these two friends were exchanged only one month before Cather's death in 1947.

Willa Cather maintained her membership in Grace Church until her death. Her letters to friends in Red Cloud include frequent inquiries about the church. On a visit to Red Cloud in 1931, she hosted a party for the Sunday School children. She regularly contributed to the financial support of the church and the guild, sometimes sending extra gifts for flowers and other needs. In 1942 Cather's donations made possible the installation of new electric lighting, and in 1946 she donated the funds for a new gas furnace.

Two of her gifts are more visible: memorial windows to her parents and to the Rev. John Mallory Bates. All of the stained glass in Grace Church is lovely, but Cather pilgrims particularly admire the Good Shepherd window in memory of her father (he had been a sheep rancher in Virginia) and the Nativity window in memory of her mother. The altar rail at Grace Church is in memory of Willa's brother Douglas. Cather and her friend Carrie Miner Sherwood gave the window above the altar in memory of the Rev. Bates. It was during the Rev. Bates's tenure that the Cather family became active in Grace Church. (The Very Rev. George H. Peek, then Dean of St. Mark's Pro-Cathedral, father of the son who preached the homilies in this booklet, officiated at the funeral of Carrie Miner Sherwood.)

Index

[Biblical References, Cather Stories and Characters, General Topics, Individuals and Organizations, Religious Topics, Themes]

Biblical references

Abram, Abraham 96, 107
Acts 47, 87, 88
Annas 55
Bethsaida 38
Caiaphas 55
Christ 35, 39, 41, 47, 51, 54, 59, 79, 81, 82, 92
Corinthians 117, 119
Daniel 101
Ezekiel 115
Garden of Eden 100, 114
Garden of Gethsemane 100
Genesis 91, 100, 107, 125
Elisha 91
Elijah 91
Hebrew, Jew, Jewish, Israel 36, 48, 58, 65, 70, 71, 87-8, 91, 96, 100, 101, 109, 114, 119, 125
Hebrews (book) 110
Herod 55
Isaiah 33, 101, 125
Jesus 36, 39, 47-8, 50-4, 59, 80, 82, 87, 91-2, 95-6, 101, 107-8, 114, 116, 119
Job 72
Joel 88
John, I John 33, 34, 51-3, 60-2, 69-70, 82, 87-8, 115, 117
Jordan 55-7
Joseph (Genesis) 70-2
Judea 55
Kings 92, 120
Kings (Magi) 79
Lamb of God 60, 101
Lazarus 52
Maccabees 59
Martha 52

Mark 38, 39, 92, 96, 118
Mary 52
Matthew 33, 38, 98, 109
Messiah 47
Paul 57, 82, 86-8, 101, 107, 118, 120, 122
Peter 32, 53
Philippians 56
Promised Land 56
Psalms 45, 69, 70, 79, 87, 92, 96, 100, 119, 120, 125
Revelation 58-60, 82
Romans 86
Samuel 118-20
Thomas 51-3
Tiberius Caesar 55
Torah 46
Tower of Babel 100
Zechariah 55

Cather stories and characters

A Lost Lady 31, 38-40, 98, 133
Ácoma 42
Adolph 39
Alexandra Bergson 103
April Twilights 98
Auclair family 90-91
Aunt Till 56
Bishop Latour 44, 62-3, 122
Burden family 31, 34-5, 51, 54, 70
Collected Stories 49
Death Comes for the Archbishop 43-44, 46, 50, 60, 87, 121
Dillon, T.E. 31
"The Enchanted Bluff" 73
"Erik Hermannson's Soul" 54
Fr. Joseph Vaillant 43, 121
Captain Daniel Forrester 38-40
Garber family 133
Godfrey St. Peter 59-61, 121
Harvey Merrick 48
Herr Wunsch 106

Ivy Peters, Poison Ivy 31, 39-40, 77
The Professor's House 121
Jim Laird 48
Marian Forrester 31, 133
My Ántonia 31, 34, 41, 51, 53, 70, 77, 86, 106, 109, 129
"Neighbor Rosicky" 84
Niel Herbert 38-9
Novel d'meuble 111
"Old Mrs. Harris" 31
Omnes Optima Fugit 50
O Pioneers! 50, 77, 105-6, 109-10, 115, 118
Panther Canyon 104
Pierre Charron 102
Roddy Blake 61
Ray Kennedy 108
Sapphira and the Slave Girl 56-7, 61
Shimerda family 34
Thea Kronberg 93, 116
Tom Outland 61, 70
"Two Friends" 31, 91
Victoria Templeton 31
Trueman, J. H. 31, 49, 109
Wick Cutter 31

General topics
Afghanistan 65
Arizona 106, 112
"As I Grow Older" 55
Colorado 94, 106
Drew University 111
Cather Project 111
Everyman, Everywoman 91
Grand Manan 126
Greenwich Village 35
"Guernica" 76
Kosovo 65
LGBT 115
Nature Conservancy 129-30
Navajo 61, 115
Nebraska 50, 105, 112, 119, 129, 133

Nebraska Public Television 16
New Mexico 61, 106
New York 27, 52-4, 79, 99, 109, 113, 129, 133
New York Times 117
Paris 115
"Prairie Fire" 98
Quebec 91, 105, 112
Red Cloud Chief 56-8
Romanticism 90
Somalia 65
University of Nebraska 16

Individuals and organizations
Abbey, Edward 114
Adrian, Gilbert 129
Albertini, Virgil 17, 111
Andrews, A. P. 121
Armagost, Jason 112
Bailey, Kenneth 95
Bair, Julene 115-6
Baker, Bruce 17, 110
Barker, The Rt. Rev. J. Scott 117
Bass, Rick 114
Bates, The Rev. John Mallory 109, 133
Beecher, The Rt. Rev. George Allen 34, 45-6, 109, 133
Beechley, Bill 129
Bennett, Mildred 16, 45, 111, 118, 129
Berry, Wendell 114
Bohlke, The Rev. Dr. L. Brent 16, 19, 45, 52, 120
Breadloaf 16
Breton, Jules ("Song of the Lark") 126
Brubeck, Dave 64
Burnett, The Rt. Rev. Joe 17, 117
Campbell, Joseph 82
Canfield, Dorothy (Fisher) 97, 116
Cartwright, Michael 119
Cather Foundation, Willa Cather Pioneer Memorial and Educational
    Foundation 17-8, 36, 44, 71, 75, 78, 88, 95, 127-8
Chane, The Rev. John Bryan 93
Clarkson, The Rt Rev. Robert Harper 17, 109

Collins, Billie 112
Conors, Don 16
Cooper, Beverly 16, 20, 55, 58
Couric, Katie 112
Darby, John Nelson 53
Day, George 15, 17
Dillard, Annie 41
Dostoyevsky, Fyodor 112
Eifler, Mark 130
Eliot, T. S. 109
English, John 20, 118
Embury, Stuart 48-9
Falwell, Jerry 101
Faulkner, William 32, 58, 77, 98, 112
Faulkner, Virginia 16
Fisher-Wirth, Ann 129
Fitzgibbon, Jim 110, 129-30
Fort, Charles 101-2
Fosdick, Henry Emerson 53-4
Frost, Robert 101-2
Funda, Evelyn 17
Gallagher, Tom 17, 110
Gandhi 53
Gere, Ellen and Mariel epigrams, 113
Geyer, Joel 110
Griswold, The Most Rev. Frank 16, 20, 80
Haller, Evelyn 17
Harris, Richard 17
Harrison, Jim 112
Heenan, The Rev. Jane 19
Heller, Joseph 78
Hemingway, Ernest 77
Homestead, Melissa 111
Hoschouer, Charlene and Doug 124-5
Hull, Ron 16, 111
Illian, Mark 129
Jaynes, The Revs. Larry and Ruth 19, 72
Jenkinson, Clay 116-7
Jewell, Andrew 17, 35, 111
Johanningsmeier, Charles 17

Kelliher, Fr. Charles 19
Kierkegaard, Soren 45
King, Martin Luther Jr. 53
Kloefkorn, Bill 101
Knoll, Robert 17
Kooser, Ted 112
Kort, Betty 16-7, 110
LaFarge, John 35, 53
Lauritzen family 17
Leak, Wade 17
Leopold, Aldo 105
Levy, Leslie 110
Lewis, C. S. 68, 87
Li, Jing 130
Linnerman, Duane 130
Lloyd, Darrel 17
MacDonald, George 37
Madigan, Mark 17
Mann, Thomas 69-70, 113
Marshall, E. G. 16
Machado 76
Maher, Sue 97
McCarthy, Cormac 78
McClure family 32, 77
McGuane, Thomas 114
Middleton, Jo Ann 82
Mignon, Charles 17
Milligan, Richard 17
Miner family 133
Mosely, Ann 17
Murphy, Devin 120
Murphy, John 17-8, 110, 122
Nagel, Hal 131
Nebraska State Historical Society 18
Obitz, Harry 16
O'Brien, Dan 104-5
Olson, Ashley 17
Olson, Paul 17, 84
Palmer, Daryl 118
Peckinpah, Sam 78

Penn, William 31-2
Pavelka, Annie 16, 108
Peek, Dorothy (Dot) 80
Peek, The Very Rev. George H. Peek 133
Picasso, Pablo 85
Porter, David 97, 110
Rauschenbusch, Walter 53
Reynolds, Guy 17, 110
Romines, Ann 17, 110
Romines, Marilyn 17
Rosowski, Sue 17, 110
Ryan, Fr. Steve 16
Sandoz Society 119
Scofield, C. I. 53
Sergeant, Elizabeth Shipley 117
Shakespeare, William 46, 71
Sherwood family 18, 133
Shively, Steve 17, 51, 93, 96, 99, 110, 118
Simcox, Carroll 34
Sister Hannah 133
Skaggs, Merrill 17, 110
Skov, Leonard 130
Slote, Dr. Berenice 16-7, 110
Smith, Dave 129
Smith, Henry Nash 106
Smith, Richard Norton 118
Southwick, Helen Cather 124-5
Southwick, Jim 125
Sprague, Barbara 16, 19, 72, 118
Springer, Joe 118
St. Exupery, Antoine de 114
Stauffer, Dr. Helen 16, 130
Stout, Janis 17, 35, 110
Strickland, Joe 129
Swift, Cheryl 129
Swift, John 16, 129
Taylor, Barbara Brown 95
Theye, Larry and Betty Becker 16
Thoreau, Henry David 72
Tillich, Paul 123

Toges, Dean 114
Tolkein, J. R. R 86
Tolstoy, Leo 33, 112
Trout, Steve 17
Tucker, Tracy 17
Turgenev, Ivan 112
Turner, Frederick Jackson 107
Tutu, The Most Rev. Desmond 53
Urgo, Joe 17, 72
Webb, Walter Prescott 105
Westerfield, Nancy 72
Western Literature Association 45
White, Frank and Charlotte 20
Whitman, Walt 34, 99
Wilson, Dennis and Cheryl 17
Wittgenstein, Ludwig 46, 100
Woods family 129
Wordsworth, William 129
Yeats, W. B. 36
Yost family 17, 110

Religious topics
Advent 55, 79
All Souls Day 47
Amish 72
Angelus 102, 121-3
Anglican, Episcopalian, Episcopal 34, 35, 47, 55, 81, 96, 101, 114, 133
Apostle 16, 90
Archbishop Temple 56
Ascension 35, 53-4, 79, 109
Baptism 34, 56, 133
Baptists 46, 101
Blessing, blessings 95-6, 108
Book of Common Prayer 34, 70, 80, 103, 115
Cathedral 44, 61, 110, 115
Cathedral of St. John the Divine 123
Christmas 46, 63, 65, 77, 80, 86, 120
Church of the Ascension 35, 53-4, 79, 114
Confirmation 34, 114, 133

Creation 84, 101, 114-5, 121
Diocese of Nebraska 17-8, 118
Divine, divinity 61, 101, 116, 120, 123
Easter 46-7, 51, 54, 56, 71, 82-4, 86, 96
Eden, New Eden 90, 100, 117, 119
Episcopalians, Episcopal, Anglican 34, 36, 47, 55, 80, 94, 101, 114, 133
Eternity 80, 116, 119, 122-3
Hanukkah 59
Miracle 49, 66, 122, 123
Moslem, Moors 121
Parish, parishioner 53, 65, 109, 115
Pentecost 87-90
Promised Land, promise 56, 86
Quran 100
Redeem, salvation 46, 71, 124, 126
Rogation 115
Roman Catholicism 47, 50, 103
Sacraments 93, 120
Salvation, redeem 47, 71, 124, 126
Seder 71
Shakers 72
Social Gospel 35, 53-4
Sower Award 17, 118
Spirit, spiritual, spirituality 20, 32, 32, 44, 45, 48, 51, 69, 73, 80, 87, 88, 89, 91, 92, 94, 96, 85, 96, 100, 102, 105, 106, 107, 109, 114, 116
St. Juliana Choir, Church 16, 20, 118
St. Mark's Pro-Cathedral 18, 118, 133
St. Theresa 64
Temple 58-9, 115
Trinity, Father, Son, Holy Ghost, Holy Spirit 35, 47, 86
Upanishads 100
Washington National Cathedral 94

Themes
America, country, nation 31, 32, 34, 46, 54, 62, 64, 72, 74, 84, 105, 106, 107, 110, 115, 118, 121, 122
Artists, artistry 115, 122
Awe, mystery, wonder 72, 73, 101, 111

Beauty 20, 37, 46, 48, 76, 78, 79, 80, 100, 103, 118, 123
Belief, believe, believing 47, 48, 50, 54, 57, 64, 65, 67, 77, 82, 86, 88, 91, 100, 115, 121, 126
Blindness, seeing, sight, vision (optical) 31, 38, 40, 41, 50, 51, 73, 90, 94, 96, 98, 119
Celebration 16, 17, 19, 31, 36, 45, 55, 59, 72, 76, 84, 86, 88, 94, 96, 99, 105, 120, 121, 124, 129, 133
Childhood, family, parenting 31, 46, 56, 60, 73, 77, 94, 102, 105, 114, 120, 124, 125, 127, 129, 133
Chronicle, narrative, tale 56, 71, 72, 79, 84, 96, 115
Clothes, garments, vestments 52, 76, 79, 80, 88, 93, 94
Country, America, nation 31, 32, 34, 44, 53, 62, 64, 72, 75, 83, 105, 106, 108, 110, 115, 118, 120, 121
Country vs town 40, 41, 56, 79, 80, 93, 109, 117
Courage, daring, risk 32, 76, 82, 83, 84, 85, 90, 91
Daring, courage, risk 32, 76, 82, 83, 84, 85, 90, 91
Death, dying 32, 36, 38, 44, 56, 60, 81, 82, 84, 85, 90, 99, 101, 102, 119, 133
Dignity, Noble 38, 54
Dreams, visions 35, 44, 48, 55, 59, 60, 70, 72, 73, 74, 83, 87, 88, 90, 91, 105, 116, 120, 123, 129
Economics and Politics 36, 80, 96, 118, 119, 121
Education, learner, school, teacher, university 16, 31, 35, 48, 50, 56, 61, 69, 71, 73, 110, 119, 127, 129, 130 133
Environment, nature 39, 46, 71, 73, 96, 112, 113, 115, 116, 119, 120, 121
Epiphany (realization) 82
Ethics, morals, morality 40, 45, 48, 65, 114
Europe, Greco-Roman world, Western World 44, 47, 82, 87, 89
Garments, clothes, vestments 53, 76, 79, 80, 88, 93, 94
Greco-Roman world, Western Civilization, Europe 44, 47, 82, 87, 90
Family, childhood, parenting 31, 45, 56, 60, 73, 74, 95, 103, 105, 113, 120, 124, 125, 126, 129, 133
Feeding 40, 88, 95
Fight, striving, struggle 48, 59, 70, 72, 88, 108
Figurative language, figure of speech, poetic figure 40, 41, 56, 84, 97, 100, 101, 103, 126
France 61
Freedom 38, 70, 74

Frontier, Pioneer, West, Southwest 33, 37, 38, 42, 43, 44, 73, 74, 90, 91, 105, 106, 107, 109, 110, 112
Garments, clothes, vestments 53, 76, 79, 80, 88, 93, 94
Geography 72, 89, 105
Goodness 35, 37, 79, 100, 123
Grace (other than Grace Church) 20, 71, 76, 78, 93, 117
Happiness 51, 54, 121, 129
Harmony 54
Holy, holiness, sacred 39, 92, 94, 100, 112, 115, 119, 120
Hospitality 16, 96
Humility, humble 54, 126
Hunger, longing, need, yearning 34, 41, 46, 57, 60, 66, 73, 79, 90, 92, 97, 101, 109, 112, 115, 117, 118, 121, 133
Ideals, idealism 40, 72, 107, 108, 120
Imagination 37, 56, 72, 73, 79, 88, 106, 112, 116, 128
Insight 17, 41, 48, 58, 73, 129
Judgment 44, 45, 46
Learner, education, school, teacher, university 16, 31, 36, 48, 49, 56, 61, 69, 71, 73, 110, 119, 129, 130, 131, 133
Longing, hunger, need, yearning 34, 41, 46, 60, 63, 69, 71, 73, 79, 89, 92, 97, 101, 109, 112, 115, 117, 118, 121, 133
Love 16, 20, 34, 35, 37, 41, 45, 47, 53, 56, 60, 62, 81, 97, 101, 117, 119, 121, 122, 127
Men and women 39, 48, 72, 74, 77, 80, 84, 84
Morals, morality, ethics 39, 47, 48, 65, 114
Mystery, awe, wonder 72, 73, 101, 114
Narrative, chronicle, tale 56, 72, 74, 79, 85, 97, 115
Nation, America, country 31, 32, 33, 44, 54, 62, 63, 72, 75, 83, 105, 106, 108, 111, 115, 118, 120, 121
Nature, environment 39, 46, 71, 74, 96, 112, 113, 115, 116, 119, 129, 130
Need, hunger, longing, yearning 34, 41, 46, 60, 63, 69, 71, 73, 79, 89, 92, 97, 101, 109, 112, 115, 117, 118, 121, 133
Noble, dignity 38, 54
Parenting, childhood, family 31, 46, 56, 60, 73, 77, 94, 102, 105, 114, 120, 124, 125, 127, 129, 133
Passion, zeal 48, 49, 52, 96, 114
Peace 81, 116
Pioneer, frontier, West, Southwest 33, 37, 38, 42, 43, 44, 73, 74, 90, 91, 105, 106, 107, 109, 110, 112

Plenty (plenitude) 49, 79, 116
Poetic figure, figurative language, figure of speech 40, 41, 56, 84, 97, 100, 101, 103, 126
Politics and Economics 36, 80, 96, 118, 119, 121
Prairie 32, 45, 48, 98, 111, 112, 114, 129-30
Prejudice 65-6
Providence 112, 115
Risk, daring, courage 32, 76, 82, 83, 84, 85, 90, 91
Romanticism 72
Sacred, holy, holiness 39, 92, 94, 100, 112, 115, 119, 120
School, education, learner, teacher, university 16, 31, 35, 48, 50, 56, 61, 69, 71, 73, 110, 119, 127, 129, 130, 133
Sight, seeing, blindness, vision (optical) 31, 38, 40, 41, 50, 51, 73, 90, 94, 96, 98, 119
Silence (stillness), 45-6, 81
Southwest, frontier, pioneer, West 33, 37, 38, 42, 43, 44, 73, 74, 90, 91, 105, 106, 107, 109, 110, 112
Spain, Spanish 43, 44, 76, 121
Striving, fight, struggle 48, 59, 70, 72, 88, 108
Tale, chronicle, narrative 56, 71, 72, 79, 84, 96, 115
Teacher, education, learner, school, university 8, 24, 27, 38, 39, 44, 48, 54, 56, 58, 89, 96, 102, 104, 105, 107
Truth epigrams, 11, 24-28, 35, 36, 38, 40, 43, 44, 46, 47, 62, 63, 65, 69, 70, 71, 72, 81, 82, 86, 91
Tolerance 26, 34, 42, 91
Town vis country 30, 31, 43, 62, 63, 74, 88, 94
Ugliness 28, 60, 62
University, education, learner, school, teacher 16, 31, 35, 48, 50, 56, 61, 69, 71, 73, 110, 119, 127, 129, 130, 133
Vestments, clothes, garments 53, 76, 79, 80, 88, 93, 94
Visions, dreams 35, 44, 48, 55, 59, 60, 70, 72, 73, 74, 83, 87, 88, 90, 91, 105, 116, 120, 123, 129
Vision (optical), blindness, seeing, sight 31, 38, 40, 41, 50, 51, 73, 90, 94, 96, 98, 119
West, frontier, pioneer, Southwest 33, 37, 38, 42, 43, 44, 73, 74, 90, 91, 105, 106, 107, 109, 110, 112
Western World, Europe, Greco-Roman World 44, 47, 82, 87, 90
Whole, wholeness, completeness 32, 44, 51, 53, 55, 56, 57, 67, 70, 71, 73, 84, 88, 97, 116, 117, 119, 120, 121

Wilderness 55, 86, 89, 91, 96, 113, 131
Witness, speak out, speak up 20, 31, 32, 35, 83, 85, 99, 100, 114
Women and men 39, 48, 72, 74, 77, 80, 84, 84
Wonder, awe, mystery 72, 73, 101, 114
Yearning, hunger, longing, need 34, 41, 46, 60, 63, 69, 71, 73, 79, 89, 92, 97, 101, 109, 112, 115, 117, 118, 121, 133
Zeal, passion 48, 49, 52, 96, 114

Willa Cather

www.ingramcontent.com/pod-product-compliance
Lightning Source LLC
Chambersburg PA
CBHW052137110526
44591CB00012B/1758